BEFORE THE CALM

John Bielinski, Jr., MS

BEFORE THE CALM

How My Mistakes
Unearthed the Real Me

Writers of the Round Table Press
PO Box 511, Highland Park, IL 60035
www.roundtablecompanies.com

Publisher: **Corey Michael Blake**
President: **Kristin Westberg**
Executive Editors: **Katherine Catmull, Aleksandra Corwin**
Editor: **Sarah Morrison**
Writer: **Geoff Campbell**
Designers: **Christy Bui, Sunny DiMartino**
Facts Keeper: **Mike Winicour**
Proofreaders: **Gary Fetters, Adam Lawrence**
Project Manager: **Leeann Sanders**
Print and Digital Post Production: **Sunny DiMartino**

Printed in the United States of America

First Edition: August 2017
10 9 8 7 6 5 4 3 2 1

Library of Congress Cataloging-in-Publication Data
Bielinski, Jr., John.
Before the calm: how my mistakes unearthed the real me /
John Bielinski, Jr.—1st ed. p. cm.
ISBN Paperback: 978-1-939418-96-8
ISBN Digital: 978-1-939418-97-5
Library of Congress Control Number: 2017947521

RTC Publishing is an imprint of Writers of the Round Table, Inc.
Writers of the Round Table Press and the RTC Publishing logo
are trademarks of Writers of the Round Table, Inc.

Disclaimer: Some names and identifying details have been
changed to protect the identities of the people involved.

To my wife Michelle—*an incredible woman*
who didn't expect the roller coaster.
(She thought she was getting on a merry-go-round.)

Also to Charles W. Beinhauer.
Thank you for sharing your experience, strength, and
hope about navigating this road of happy destiny.

Contents

Foreword

This is a book written by a man who knows his own story.

It was not always so. When I met John seven years ago, we were both playing the same game, relying upon all the usual scripts: the career path script, the relationship script, the education script—those stories we tell others to feed our own egos, complete with the impressive catalogue of our humble accomplishments.

The problem was, our stories—our scripts—were bullshit. We were about to slam headfirst into that realization.

I watched John struggle when he reached the point in his life when all his stories crumbled. After a lifetime of self-deception piled on half-truths and lies, John, like countless others who carry similar demons, came face-to-face with the truth after crushing life events provided him with a glimpse of his real story, of his reality.

People who have been through the fire like this can then unearth their entire real story—provided they're willing to face many ugly and painful truths. Chief among those is that guys like us have no idea how this all happened. We don't know our own story.

John was willing to pay that price, to bear that pain. The result is an amazing life—not built on his own with the fruit of his own skills and ideas, but constructed by casting aside everything he thought he knew. It was only when he realized he didn't have the answers that he began the process of recovery.

The situation John and I found ourselves in is hardly unique. And thankfully, we aren't outliers in our ability to transcend our pasts. But for both of us, it was hearing the life stories—the real life stories—of others that enabled us to understand what we faced and what we needed to do. Hearing others describe the truth about their own lives helped us to access the real details of our own stories, giving our lives new meaning.

John's book is a gift to those who've reached their own bottom, to those struggling with the realization that their stories have failed them. By sharing his journey with honesty and humanity, John blazes a path for all who need help in finding the truths of their own stories.

Sean Honan
Founder of Honcho's Holdings LLC
A Buffalo, NY–based REIT
June 2017

Prologue

The police headquarters in Tonawanda, New York: a large brick building taking up a whole city block, with a US flag flying next to the front door. Inside, the cold, sterile brightness of fluorescent lights. Every thought seems like a scream.

I see a bleary-eyed man who looks like he's losing his life. Something about him touches my heart—compassion. And then I understand it's me, my reflection in the observation glass. I close my eyes and shudder. I'm fucked.

My phone call: on the other end of the line, a friendly voice that twists to sound unfriendly. "Don't bother coming home," my wife says.

"You don't understand," I say. "I'm in jail."

The past months—no, years, I've spent years like this—they come crashing over and around me like a storm that's finally broken. It's all raining down on me:

the noisy performances, rattling off reassuring, self-aggrandizing lines I'd memorized—lines that do me no good now, here. Then the ominous silences where conversations should have been. Most of all the chaos, the wild destruction, the numbness of the drinking.

It wasn't me. That had always been my mantra.

It was never me. I was never to blame.

I was quick with words and always had a stooge for the trouble I got myself into. I always had an angle.

I look out from behind prison bars and wonder how it has come to this.

Who have I become?

Is it too late to stop this storm from destroying my life?

Is it too late to become somebody else?

Chapter 1

Fight or Flight

When I was five years old, I started a rock fight with the teenage paperboy. One of my earliest memories is of being shocked when one of his rocks hit me square in the forehead. I gently brought my hand to my face, feeling the hot liquid streaming down my cheeks, and then I saw it there, all over my hand: *blood.* In the ER, they wrapped me in a sheet to restrain me while they stitched up the wound.

Pain and fear are nature's great teachers—*that dog growled at you, so you should be afraid of it.* And then, once you are afraid, you have two choices.

You can run away, or you can fight.

It was an important lesson for me, though I didn't learn it all at once; it settled on me over time. Because while life eventually threw plenty of metaphorical rocks in my face, the early part of my childhood probably looked from the outside like a Norman Rockwell painting. And sometimes that's how it felt, too.

Hamburg, New York, is a quintessential small town on the outskirts of Buffalo, and our house was one of the most impressive homes on our suburban street. It had nooks and crannies and plenty of space to be a kid without disturbing the business of the household. I remember the distinctive woodwork in that house; my mom painstakingly removed layers of paint to reveal beautiful wood, its grain highlighted by the light stain she applied. One room had a colorful sunset wallpapered onto a full wall, floor to ceiling. We called it "the Florida room," and during cold, gray New York winters we would gaze at it, imagining we were basking on a sandy beach. We had a giant wood-burning fireplace in the living room, and near it a sturdy round oak table where my dad taught me chess and would sometimes play with me after dinner.

Our basement was so large that we could play roller hockey and hide-and-go-seek there. In our backyard stood a horse-chestnut tree, a source of fascination and treats: the tree bore strange, spiky green shells you could peel back to reveal a nut. The backyard blended into an open field, where Dad would sometimes hit me grounders and pop flies.

It was in that backyard, accompanied by the cicadas' songs on warm summer nights, that I started my first business. My father taught me how to hunt for night crawlers—simple earthworms—and I sold them for a dollar a dozen. Dad even bought me a refrigerator to store my stock and a miner's helmet with a headlamp to leave my hands free for the business of catching worms. He also helped me in my second business, snow blowing. Dad taught me how to use our snowblower, and once I plowed our driveway, I could travel around the neighborhood offering my services. Given that Buffalo gets nearly a hundred inches of snow every winter, I did pretty good business.

When I was just six or seven, my dad and I were driving down a dirt road on a fishing trip. My dad suddenly brought the car to a stop. The tires crunched on the gravel, and the billowing cloud of dust that had been trailing us rushed past us like a ghost.

"Come on over here," Dad said, helping me get on his lap. "You want to drive?"

"Yes!"

He gave the car a little gas as I began steering, suddenly aware that driving wasn't quite as easy as it looked. As we drove past a small hill on the right, the car veered in that direction. "Oh, you better turn or we'll drive up the hill," Dad said.

Just in the nick of time—as usual for me, all my life—I steered straight.

That day Dad and I fished together, sitting quietly by Lake Kirsty, dragonflies skimming the surface of the water. We snacked on Dad's infamous trick bologna sandwiches, where he cut the pieces of bread in half but not the meat. I would try to pick up one half of the sandwich and smile, rolling my eyes, when the two halves stuck together. As always, my dad asked me to hold his pole for him for a minute, and when I took it, a fish already hung on the line, just waiting for me to reel it in.

One time I came home to find that my mom had transformed my bedroom into a jungle with a mural painted on two large rectangles of plywood. My jaw dropped when I saw the lush green backdrop framing my bed and the netting in the corner.

"You like it?" Mom asked. She stepped back to survey her handiwork, tucking her shoulder-length brown hair behind her ears.

"Yes!" I exclaimed. Grinning, I ran my eyes over the scene: tigers, elephants, a giraffe—and a deer. I laughed. "Deer don't live in the jungle," I protested.

She laughed. "Yeah, well, they do now."

On Sundays, we went to church together at Saints Peter and Paul, a large brick Roman Catholic church with two soaring spires framing an elaborate rose window. My older sister Lisa, my younger brother Billy, and I sat together on the pew, flanked by our parents, all of us wearing our Sunday best. Sometimes our family brought up the offering, which seemed like a great honor.

Mom was active in the PTA, Cub Scouts, and the welcome wagon committee for new families that moved to our neighborhood. She was the hostess who organized our annual Fourth of July neighborhood party, camping events for the local kids, and football parties in the fall.

But Christmas was my favorite time of the year. My mother made Christmas magical: the individualized handmade Christmas stockings, the painted plywood cutouts of Santa and his elves she crafted for the front yard. The tree, shimmering with ornaments and lights, stood nestled in a blanket of glittering snow, a model train circling its base. And underneath the tree was a mountain of gifts, presents enough for a family of ten. I gasped when I got my figure-eight racetrack with two cars—one cop and one robber.

But Christmas was so much more than gifts and glitz. It was the warmth of having us all together. It was the family dinner of fondue, the smile that spread across Mom's face when we laughed.

. . .

But the reality is that surface appearances can be deceiving. If you watch a duck float on a pond, you might think it looks peaceful—until you look more closely and see its feet paddling furiously. No one lives in a Norman Rockwell painting; life is more complicated than that.

My father grew up in a rough Buffalo neighborhood with strict Polish parents, the kind who didn't think feelings were worth talking about. So my dad was the same way—brusque, strict, not the kind of man to express emotion, not the kind of dad to say he loved us.

One morning when I was around five years old, he called me to the kitchen and asked me to sit down at the yellow, cracked-ice Formica table where we took many of our meals. Dad, who didn't smoke, lit a cigarette and laid it in the notch of an ashtray. "Johnny, take a puff," he said.

I brought the cigarette to my mouth and inhaled deeply, as I'd seen Mom do. I gagged on the hot, acrid smoke and went into a three-minute coughing jag, the room seeming to swim around me. "You don't like it—good," Dad said when I finally stopped hacking.

Then he poured a glass of whiskey. "Have a drink of this," he said, pushing the glass toward me. I brought the glass to my mouth as though it was soda or milk, drinking too fast to be overwhelmed by the harsh smell. A searing heat washed over my tongue and down my throat. It felt like a fire had broken out in my stomach. I coughed and gagged again.

I stared at my father in disbelief. Parents were supposed to protect their children, not encourage them to do things that could hurt them. But as his lips curled into a slight smile, I realized even at my young age that Dad was trying to protect me. Closing my eyes tight to keep the room from spinning, I decided one thing: smoking and drinking weren't for kids.

Dad was an optometrist, and he built an office on the side of our house where he would work and see patients. He always had an intense work ethic and was driven largely by his practice, which took up most of his time and energy. During my baseball games, I scanned the bleachers for him, but he rarely came to watch me. And he never knew what Mom had gotten us for Christmas.

Yet I believed I was his favorite. He treated me just a little differently than he treated Lisa and Billy, gave me just slightly more attention. I worked hard for his approval—memorizing the times tables he quizzed me on during car rides, trying to beat him at chess, playing baseball because he liked it, trying to be a wise guy like him.

Lisa, two years older than me, was busy with her own life and friends. She took after my mom: she had shoulder-length brown hair and was self-conscious about her weight. She was a tough girl, not afraid to beat me up if she felt I deserved it. Billy was always ahead of the game. He was great at sports, almost as good as I was despite being four years younger, and he was a good-looking kid who drew people to him.

I was part of this family. But somehow, I never felt like I belonged. As I grew up I felt increasingly like an outsider, a peripheral student, a peripheral person. I felt like I was always trying to prove myself.

Pleasant Avenue Elementary School was anything but pleasant for me. I couldn't make myself pay attention to the readings and exercises, and words often swam before me, refusing to become clear. I started getting pulled out to attend special education classes. When I waited in the hallway with the other kids who needed supplemental learning, my cheeks grew hot and I stared at the floor.

One day in my regular class, we went around the room reading sections of a story aloud. My stomach tightened when it was my turn to read. The story involved someone named Jon, without an "h," but I kept reading the name as *Joan*. Over and over, the teacher corrected me. "John, that's *Jon*," she said. My heart was beating like a drum, and I could feel the blood rushing to my face. I heard the other students waiting and shifting in their seats. I felt stuck in time. *But my name is John*, I thought. *Not Joan. Why doesn't this make any sense?*

There was one bright spot for me at Pleasant, and that was my second-grade teacher, Mr. Black. He was the first male teacher I'd ever had, and I remember fearing him at first. There were rumors that he was mean, and I got physically ill when I learned I'd be in his class.

He did turn out to be a hard teacher. But he was fair, he listened to me, and he embraced creative learning.

I remember returning to Mr. Black's class after spending an hour in one of the special classes I had to take. He greeted me by telling me that I was still responsible for work the rest of the class had done while I was gone.

"That's not fair," I said.

"What do you mean?"

"I have work in this other class, and if I have to do what I missed in this class, I have more work than everybody else."

To my astonishment, he paused for a moment, then said, "You've got a point. I'll adjust your workload." He was probably the first teacher I ever had who'd really listened to me.

And he taught us far more than academics. I remember one of my classmates wet himself. Mr. Black noticed before any of the other kids could say something. "It looks like something spilled out of your lunchbox," Mr. Black said casually to the student. "Why don't you go to the bathroom and wash up, and I'll clean up this spill."

When the student left the room, Mr. Black fixed us with an icy stare. We all knew the truth. "If you make fun of him, you're all going to get it," he yelled. He allowed this student to save face, and that made a big impression on me, one that I would carry with me into my own work much later.

But not even Mr. Black could help me make sense of my world or sort out my motivations. For example, sometimes I lied for no real reason, at least not that I understood at the time. I now think I most likely lied to make myself feel important. For example, I liked to make bows and arrows, and I told my friend Kevin I was so good at it because I was part Native American. The next day he scowled at me and said, "My mom said you're *obviously* not Native American."

"Yes, I am," I shot back, "and you're *obviously* a pussy."

Other times I lied with a purpose. I remember stealing money from my mother's purse and hiding it outside so I could pretend I found it. I remember calling our house phone from my father's office line to say Sunday school had been canceled.

I even lied in confession, telling the priest I'd said bad words or hadn't listened to my parents. I'm not sure why I did it; I did plenty of things that I could have confessed. I guess I just didn't want to really think about my behavior and own my mistakes. My way was easier; after reciting the prescribed number of Hail Marys, I was on my way.

Church didn't make much sense to me. I remember being confused by the part of Mass where everyone stood and recited the Lord's Prayer. *Our Father, who art in heaven, hallowed be thy name.* I didn't know what "hallowed" meant or why we were saying these words in unison. So I would daydream and study the dust motes floating in the light—muted indigo, crimson, and amber—filtering through the stained-glass windows.

I have a vivid memory of walking down our driveway and pausing, overwhelmed. I can't remember exactly what I'd just done—lied, stolen, called someone a pussy. I just remember feeling a swell of conscience. I felt absolutely terrible.

I'm a bad kid, I thought. *I've got to quit being so sneaky.*

Midway through the third grade, a girl named Thea announced that her family was moving away, so our class had a big goodbye party for her. While I ate my cupcake and watched Thea smiling as she read all her goodbye cards, I thought about how nice it would be to have people miss me so much. I remembered my mom mentioning the possibility of me switching schools to help with my learning issues. If switching schools got me *this* kind of attention, I thought, it was a great idea.

So I talked with my parents, and we decided that I would transfer to the K–8 Catholic school at Saints Peter and Paul. On my last day at Pleasant Elementary, I waited patiently for the cupcakes and cards—but it was just business as usual. I have just one memory of that day. A boy named Mike approached me and said, "I always liked you, John. I'm sad to see you go, and I hope you like your new school."

My new school wasn't any better than my old one. For one thing, we had to wear uniforms I hated: blue pants, white shirt, belts, and what I considered at the time to be dress shoes. For another, it seemed like I was constantly taking standardized tests as I was evaluated for special education services—multiple-choice Scantron tests where I had to fill in the bubbles.

I remember sitting at my desk, thinking, *This sucks, this sucks. I don't want to do this.* It got to the point where I just filled in the circles without even reading the questions, just to be done with it.

I hated having to go to special education classes. One of the teachers always began class with riddles, but they were hardly mind-benders for me. She would read clearly and slowly. "Imagine you're in a new town, and you need a haircut. There are only two barbers in town: one with scraggly hair, and one who is well groomed," she said. "Which one do you go to?"

Well, of course, you go to the scraggly barber, because with only two barbers in town, they had to cut each other's hair. Day after day, I'd always have the answer almost before the teacher had finished posing the riddle.

"Are you getting these from somewhere else?" she asked one day. "It seems like you have the answer as you're walking in the door."

"No," I answered truthfully. "They just aren't very hard."

I was okay at math—though no one was suggesting I had a future at NASA—but I still had trouble reading, and I just didn't find school interesting. Sure, I could solve riddles, but it wasn't like I got a grade for that. Mostly I felt in over my head, and I never understood *why* I had to learn this or that fact. None of it made any sense to me. Traditional teaching methods bored me, and my grades showed it.

I felt stupid—but much worse, I started *believing* I was stupid.

My favorite class was gym, but we only had gym one day a week. I looked forward to it all week long.

One day during gym, while we were in the midst of a spirited basketball game, a nun pulled me out of the game. I came over, breathing hard, sweat beads popping up on my arms and legs.

"John, we need to talk about your grades," Sister said.

That's pretty much all I remember of the conversation. I stood there, my breath returning, and it was like my ears stopped working. I felt incredulous, angry. *She pulled me out of* gym *to talk about* grades? *I may be stupid, but I'm not* stupid. *I know my grades stink. We can talk about that anytime—as long as it's not during the one class I'm any good at.*

Still, I struggled with an identity: although I loved gym and was really competitive in sports, I wasn't really a jock. I wasn't a nerd, I wasn't a "bad kid" who smoked, I wasn't an artist. Where did I fit in?

Probably because I felt like such an outsider, the moments when I felt like I belonged stand out in my memory. A friend named Jeff opened my eyes to the world of imagination. When we were ten, he introduced me to Dungeons & Dragons, a fantasy role-playing game.

We played all the time. It's a game of imagination and creativity, and it's about vivid storytelling. I became good at the game and heavily invested in it. In fact, though I had difficulties reading, I was eventually reading outside of school: I was willing to read up on Dungeons & Dragons because I was motivated to learn it.

When I was twelve, I walked past the martial arts studio near our house. A wide overhead door was open, revealing the interior. Mats covered the floor, and martial artists—older than me, most of them adults—sparred with each other, their bodies moving gracefully and with great precision. I stood there transfixed.

As a little kid, my favorite show had been *Kung Fu*, with David Carradine. The show's hero, Caine, trains at a monastery to become a priest and martial arts expert, and he is a peaceful man. But when his beloved mentor is killed, Caine avenges him and then has to go into hiding. His intention is to lay low—but in every episode, bad guys do something unjust, and Caine is forced to use his kung fu and whup them.

I *loved* that stuff. I loved pretending to be a master fighter; Billy and I played a game called "foot fighting" where we would strap pillows to our feet and kick each other. I was drawn to the idea of learning to discipline and use my body. As I stood and watched the martial artists, I decided I had to try it. I marched into the dojang and walked over to a man who looked like he was a sensei. "I'd like to sign up for lessons," I said.

Right away I knew I'd found my place. It was a tae kwon do dojang, and the leader was addressed not as sensei but as *sa boo nim*—literally, teaching father. I took three classes per week, and each class was two hours long. I finally had a way to channel my tremendous energy. I soaked up the philosophy: "Until you learn to use your hands and feet," Sa Boo Nim Joe said, "you never touch a weapon." I learned the katas, sequences of moves in patterns meant to teach discipline and structure. When all the students moved through the katas together, it was like a synchronized dance. I learned quickly, and soon black belts wanted to spar with me.

My parents paid the seven dollars per week for my lessons, and my mom sometimes dropped me off for class, but otherwise they seemed uninterested in my martial arts. When I tested to go from my white belt to my yellow belt, Lisa was the only one who came.

At the end of the tests, our *sa boo nim* went down the line of students, untying the old belts, throwing them to the side, and tying on the new belts. Each time he did this, he shook the student's hand and said, "Practice harder." When he arrived in front of me, he untied my belt, launched it to the side, and tied on my new belt. He shook my hand. I waited for him to tell me I should practice harder.

"Well done," he said. My body felt like a giant smile. After the ceremony, I ran to Lisa, beaming. *I found something I'm good at.*

Around this time, our family took a vacation to a Western-style dude ranch. I should have lasting memories of riding horses and sitting around a fire under the starlight, but my most vivid memory is of what happened after the trip. Apparently, the ranch never charged Dad's credit card—but instead of calling the ranch to alert them of the error, he crowed about it. "I really pulled one over on them," he bragged. "We got a free vacation!"

I was starting to see my dad in a new light. Hearing him brag about our free trip, I felt almost proud. *That's how you have to think to get ahead*, I thought. *That's how wise guys do it. This is how you work over the world.*

In so many ways, Dad was larger than life to me. I have vivid memories of him coming home after gambling at the Knights of Columbus Hall and tossing a wad of bills into the air so the money fell like snow, telling Billy and me we could keep whatever we caught.

Partly because of my newfound appreciation for Dad's worldly ways, I didn't feel like a bad kid anymore. Instead I felt glimmers of power as I entered my teen years, like I was in control of myself and my destiny. I'd discovered something I was good at—tae kwon do. And in my Dad I'd found an example of how a man succeeds in the world. My days of feeling guilt over my sneakiness were gone. I *embraced* my sneakiness.

I started sneaking out of the house at night. I would creep out of my bedroom window and walk across the roof of my dad's office. I gripped the edge of the roof, lowered myself down against the wall, and jumped down to the soft grass.

Every time I left, I bunched up blankets and pillows to make it appear I was sleeping soundly. But I also left a note saying where I was going, just in case my parents found me out. That way I could say, "But I left a note! I didn't want you to *worry*." If I got caught, I'd have insurance.

I often snuck out to meet up with Bobby Jones, my best friend. Although I'd sneak out of the house at night to see him, Bobby and I didn't do anything particularly wrong. We just enjoyed hanging out.

Our families were close—Bobby had two younger siblings, Tina and Michael, and we would all play together while our parents drank, played bridge, and watched Buffalo Bills games. We often had backyard barbecues together.

Between the ages of thirteen and fifteen, Bobby and I became inseparable. His dad owned a lot of real estate, including a summer camp where Bobby and I went together for weeks on end. We developed buddy comedy routines, playing pranks on other campers. During free swim at the lake, Bobby would say, "When you swim to the dock, just be careful of the snapping turtles." The other campers didn't know I was lurking under the dock, waiting to pinch their toes.

We played pranks back at home, too. Once when Bob came to spend the night, we were having what we called a "ninja battle," which meant trying to throw unsharpened pencils at each other in the dark. We heard a car pull into the driveway, and then we heard the door slam: Lisa returning home from a friend's house. I heard her go into the downstairs bathroom.

I whispered to Bob, "Let's give her a scare."

Taking my cue, he tiptoed down the hallway past the bathroom. Just as I passed the door, I disguised my voice, dropping it down a few octaves. "Hey Tony," I growled menacingly, "let's go see what's in the basement."

We snickered and dashed down to the basement. Moments later, an earsplitting shriek tore through the house. Footsteps pounded overhead as Lisa ran into our parents' bedroom, yelling at the top of her lungs, "There's someone in the house! Someone's in the basement!"

The door to the basement crashed open—my father stood at the top of the staircase. He was only wearing his tighty-whities, and he brandished an unplugged lamp like a bat, ready to bash intruders' heads. "Who's there?" he bellowed.

Bobby and I crept to the bottom of the staircase, our hands in the air. "Just us, Dad. We were just playing foosball," I said meekly. But then Bob and I caught each other's eye and dissolved into laughter, and we kept on laughing even after we heard the wail of a squad car pulling into the driveway, responding to my mother's frantic 9-1-1 call.

"Jesus, Johnny," my dad said. "I should crack both your heads."

Mom pursed her lips together as Lisa snarled, "You're *jerks*."

Bobby and I often spent time at the roller rink, skating with our other friends. Several nights a week, the rink had DJs who played music as we raced and did tricks. I became a strong skater, leaning and tilting through the crowds of kids.

Then they brought roller hockey to the rink. I'd never really played hockey, but I was such a good skater that once I picked up momentum, circling the net, no one could stop me. The rink had a house league, where teams of kids our age played each other, and a traveling team called the Hamburg Psychos. Players on the Psychos were older, and they were *real* hockey players.

One of the Psychos—also the rink's main DJ—was the coach of a house team of younger kids. When my team played that team, the DJ told one of his players, a kid named Eddie, to come after me. His job was to piss me off, distract me, trip me up. At one point, I'd had enough: I stopped on a dime, whirled on Eddie, and slammed my stick straight into his face mask. I heard the whistle and sailed off to the box without a word, taking my penalty.

After the game, Rick, the DJ, came up to me. "Good game," he said, looking at me intently. "I was wondering—do you think you'd be interested in playing for the Psychos?"

I tried to stay cool. "Absolutely," I said. I felt like I was in a dream. I was going to be playing with a real team, guys who sauntered around the rink like they owned the place. It felt *awesome.*

I didn't get a ton of playing time, being one of the youngest and least experienced players. But I developed a reputation. Whenever one of our players went down or got hit, I would spring to my feet from the bench, pretending to go nuts. I would freak out, flailing with rage, about to start a bench-clearing brawl, and my teammates would play their parts in the show: "Hold him back!" "Easy, Johnny!"

I became John "The Bounty Hunter" Bielinski. At the start of games, the announcer would introduce all the players as we skated one by one onto the huge wood oval shining under the lights. "Here's John ... the *Bounty Hunter* ... Bielinski!" his voice boomed, applause swelling as I pumped my fist and flew around the rink. My chest swelled with pride.

I had martial arts, I had friends, I had roller hockey. I finally felt like I fit in. Things were going pretty great.

And then, in an instant, everything changed—everything.

One morning, Dad called a family meeting in the

kitchen. As I sat at that yellow table, I looked quizzically at Billy, sitting on the floor, and then at Lisa, perched on the counter. They seemed just as confused as I was.

And then I looked at Mom. I'll never forget her glassy eyes. It was almost like she was a wax figure, there but not there, present but someplace far away. A cigarette burned in the ashtray in front of her, but she didn't smoke it.

Is Mom sick? Does she have cancer? My imagination churned.

Finally Dad spoke, breaking the nervous silence: "I'm having an affair with Mrs. Jones."

We all stared back at him, dumbfounded. It took several moments for me to wrap my mind around what Dad was saying. He was having an affair with Bobby's mom. In the several beats of terrified silence that followed, I noticed Mom's hand shaking as she picked up her smoldering cigarette.

Chapter 2

Flashpoint

For a short period—I can't remember whether it was a few days or a few weeks—Dad stayed at the house. I don't recall whether he slept on the couch. I don't recall much of anything from that foggy period, except that I tried to talk my parents into staying together. At the worldly-wise age of fifteen, I thought I could fix this.

I found the two of them talking in my dad's office, wearing serious expressions. They glanced in my direction but didn't acknowledge me. Even without a welcome, I took a seat where patients would ordinarily sit as they discussed their eye conditions. It was up to me to save this family.

"I don't think you should get a divorce," I said. "We should try to work this out."

Mom stared blankly at my father's framed medical degree. Dad looked at me momentarily before shooting a glance at my mother. "Not now, Johnny."

My mom's mouth tightened, but she didn't say anything. She seemed far away, so distant I wasn't even sure she saw me.

My stomach drew into a knot. I didn't have the self-awareness or tools to understand their feelings, let alone mine. But I felt like a tree had fallen on my chest.

And so during that period before Dad left, my mind was always racing: *What's going to happen? How's this going to work?* And perhaps most importantly, *What does this mean for me? Us? Our family?*

Finally my dad moved out, packing boxes into his little stick-shift Subaru—the same car I'd sometimes snuck out in and driven during midnight joyrides when I was only fourteen. He went to live for a while with his parents in West Seneca, about fifteen miles away.

Lisa and Billy took Mom's side—they were furious with Dad and wanted nothing to do with him. But I was determined to get along with both Mom and Dad, so I would still get together with Dad sometimes. We'd shoot pool or play ping-pong, though playing with him wasn't usually fun for me. He couldn't bear to lose to anybody at anything. In ping-pong, he'd smash the ball so hard that it stung if it hit me.

Still, I remember I was just glad to be with him, no matter how awkward our gatherings could be. From then on, whenever I saw a father with his kids on a Saturday night, all of them tense and quiet, I understood he was probably a Weekend Dad, trying to get his dad points in. A dad like mine.

Before the divorce, Dad had taken me on a fishing

trip to Balsam Lake, where we'd goofed around together and I'd felt like we were a team. After the divorce, Dad took me and Billy on another fishing trip to Balsam Lake, but this time things were different. Billy hated fishing, and the whole vibe of the outing was sterile and forced. Billy pouted and went through the motions.

Midway through the trip, the three of us were fishing off a boat on the glassy water. Billy faced away from us, head down, lightly gripping his pole. My dad had taken off his shirt and stood in the middle of the boat in his swim trunks. I looked at Billy—his elbows rested on the side of the boat as he frowned into the water—and then at my dad. The tension in our boat overwhelmed me, and I desperately wanted things to be more lighthearted, more normal.

I caught Dad's eye and whispered, "Make some noise."

A look of confusion crossed his face, but then he smiled slyly. "Yo, ho, ho, ho!" he yelled, some kind of bizarre cross between a pirate and one of the seven dwarves. Billy shot a dark look at him before refocusing on the water's surface. "Yo, ho, ho …" Dad called again—and as he did, I silently slipped into the water.

I swam beneath the boat, through the cool dark water. Positioning myself right in front of Billy, I counted three, then rocketed myself up into the air, yelling, "Baaaaaah!"

Billy gasped and recoiled, swinging his pole at me. "Asshole!" he yelled.

My dad was laughing so hard he nearly fell out of the boat. After a few moments, Billy started laughing too. For a moment we felt like a family again.

Unfortunately, moments like that were rare.

Things were strained and different at home, too. The first Christmas after Dad left, I came home from school one day to see that Mom had put up the Christmas tree and decorations. She even had the train running around the base. Wordlessly, I put all the ornaments back into the box. When Mom came into the room, she looked at me quizzically.

"We're doing this as a family," I said.

So Mom, Lisa, Billy, and I put the decorations back up together—without talking. No Christmas carols, no hot chocolate or cookies. No fondue. At least we were together.

My mother was trying, but as time passed she started fading, withdrawing. She started going out to bars, her favorite being a country-western place called the Golden Nugget. It had a special where you could buy a glass shaped like a cowboy boot and get it filled all night. Those boot-shaped glasses started piling up around the house.

She'd thrown herself into her family, so now, with us nearly grown, she found herself adrift. After having stayed home with us for almost two decades, she returned to work as an optician, but that didn't provide a social life. She'd never had a vast network of friends. She'd had her husband and one best friend, Cindy—Mrs. Jones— and now she'd lost Dad to Cindy and Cindy to Dad.

But at the time, I didn't really understand all this. I just felt like Mom was no longer there for me.

After the divorce, I sometimes had trouble sleeping, so I would leave my bed to sleep in strange places around the house. One night, around age fifteen, I lay on the living room floor and tried to go to sleep, but my swirling thoughts kept me wide awake. *I need my dad. I need my mom. I shouldn't have to figure all this out on my own.* As my mind raced from thought to thought—worry about my fragmenting family, wonder about my identity and what my parents' breakup meant for me, confusion about these new creatures called girls and how I was supposed to navigate all the complexities of dealing with them—I noticed how still the house was. Tree branches scraped against the roof. An occasional car rumbled past the house. A clock ticked.

And then, so soft that at first I thought it was the radio, I heard my mother's muffled sobs. I closed my eyes, envisioning her face, tears running over her cheeks. I may have needed her, but she needed someone, too.

I pulled my blanket over my head.

. . .

It was around the time of my parents' divorce that I began to drink.

I'll never forget the first time. I was at the roller rink for a teen lock-in, where we would skate and stay up all night long. I was there with Billy, D. J. Krause, and Bobby Jones. Bobby and I were still best friends—we simply never talked, not a single time, about what had happened between our parents. We were regulars at the rink, and we even had choreographed skate routines that we thought made us look pretty cool—especially in front of the girls who were watching us. I loved the attention.

One night, some of these girls snuck in a bottle of rum, which we then stole from their locker. We mixed it with some Coke, and I wasn't impressed; to me it just tasted like crappy Coke. But soon I slid into a giddy, goofy drunkenness. I led my friends onto the rink. We skated around, gliding with cocky self-assurance, until I signaled to the group that we were going to do our signature coordinated 360-degree spins. Ordinarily, we did this with no problem. But tonight, we were drunk. We wiped out and laughed our asses off. Everything was warm and fun and free. I felt like I was connected to the whole world.

We started drinking occasionally, and then often. I even drank at home during sleepovers in what used to be my dad's office. We'd moved a foosball table in there, and my friends and I would play a foosball drinking game or just hang out and slam down Genny Pounders—cheap sixteen-ounce Genesee beers that my friend Scott bought with a fake ID. I remember my first bad hangover, the feeling that my insides were made of volcanic Jell-O and my head was a throbbing drum. Mom assumed I had the flu and let me sleep.

One morning a few weeks after that, she saw my blurry eyes. "Have you been *drinking*?" she asked. Something in her tone rubbed me the wrong way; wasn't she the one filling the house with those glass boots from the bar? But I didn't even need my mother's hypocrisy, as I saw it, as an excuse to lay into her. I was entering full-bore teenage rebellion. Besides, I was angry at her. I know it makes no sense, but I think I somehow blamed *her* for the divorce.

"You're so dumb, you didn't realize I was hungover the other day," I sneered. "You thought I had the flu."

My dad had always been the disciplinarian in our house, but now he was gone. What was Mom going to do to me? Her eyes narrowed to slits, and she stared at me for what seemed like minutes. Then she slammed the door to my room.

Around that time, I got invited to a hockey teammate's house to watch the Sabres play an elimination playoff game—game 7 of an NHL Stanley Cup playoff series. The Sabres lost, but three of my teammates decided they were going to greet the returning team plane that night at Prior Aviation behind the Buffalo airport.

I really needed to go home and get some sleep. I couldn't afford to stay home from school the next day— lately I'd been cutting class like it was my job. I was constantly being called to the principal's office and lying to his face, saying I had to go to funerals, wakes, and doctors' appointments. When he asked why I had to go to the doctor so often, I said I was being treated for scoliosis—years earlier I'd heard someone use the term, and I just ran with it.

I knew the team charter wouldn't be coming in until two or three in the morning. But I thought, *Fuck it. I'm going to the airport.*

So there I was with my teammates, four guys in our cool white Psychos jackets waiting in the reception area. I was in full bounty hunter mode, jumping up and down and pumped for the Sabres.

A reporter approached me. "Big fan?" he asked.

"I'm such a big fan that I told my mom I was sleeping at a friend's house," I said. "There's no way I was missing this."

He grinned. "You mind if I print this?"

"Go ahead," I said. I helpfully spelled out my name for him.

"I guess you'll be skipping school tomorrow?" he asked.

"Nah," I joked, "I'll just leave straight from the airport."

I ended up sleeping at a friend's house. The next day, somebody passed me in the hallway between classes and called out, "Saw you on the front page, Bielinski! Nice!" I assumed he was talking about the *Hamburg Bee*, but when I found a copy and skimmed through it, I didn't see my name anywhere—front page *or* inside.

Still, when I got home, I decided to play it safe and unplug all the phones. I didn't want people calling my mom once she was back from work.

When Mom got home, she slammed the door and dropped her purse with a thud on the kitchen table. As she stormed into the living room, I could tell by the heaviness of her footsteps that she was angry. She knew.

"Well," I said, "who told you?"

"Who *didn't*!?" She tossed the newspaper on a coffee table in front of me.

It turned out all of Buffalo knew I'd pulled a fast one on my mom. I'd made the front page of the *Buffalo News*.

I had two choices: I could have a shouting match with her or turn on the charm. I had something of a gift of talking my way out of trouble, so I decided to try it on Mom.

"You're right to be mad," I said. "I told the guys I needed to go home, but they insisted on going to see the Sabres. It was so late I didn't want to wake you to come get me."

"Well, you're safe—that's something," she said. "But you're still grounded."

I nodded, as if resigned. In reality, I knew she couldn't possibly enforce her punishment.

I wanted attention; I wanted to fit in; I wanted to entertain people and win their approval. The only way I could get what I wanted in school was by clowning around. I created such a distraction in my history class that the teacher eventually moved me to a seat at the front of the class by his desk. Any time he left the classroom, I'd grab his grade book and change all my grades. My classmates watched with approval. "Do mine too!"

Eventually, my friends and I decided that hanging around the roller rink was no longer cool. We'd discovered a place called S.P.I.T. (Special Place in Town), which from Monday through Saturday was a bustling bar. On Sundays only, S.P.I.T. became a dry bar and they let teens in, making it the most popular spot in Buffalo for kids to hang out.

One night, three friends and I decided to enter a lip-sync contest. While we were up in front of the crowd, lip syncing and pretending to play our instruments, everyone roared with applause. This was *fun*. We became a formal lip-sync band—Visions. The kids at the nightclub loved us. I'd be at the mall, and people would say, "You're in Visions! I love you guys!" Girls would ask us for autographs. I felt like I was in a boy band. I took to wearing a black trench coat, and I sported a mullet with bleached stripes down the sides. I walked around in a cloud of Brut cologne.

I continued drinking, although not usually in the club. We usually just drank before we got there. Once I was buzzed, I was comfortable exploring my inability to dance.

It seemed like the better things got in my social life, the worse they got at home. Mom and I seemed to argue about everything now. Eventually, I decided I'd have fewer fireworks with Dad, who now had his own apartment and had offered to let me move in with him.

It was a sterile place, a typical two-bedroom apartment. The walls were bare, and he had no photos of Lisa, Billy, or me. The bookshelves held mostly books about gambling—books on how to beat the dealer.

Part of the appeal of living with my dad was that while Mom was totally opposed to me getting a motorcycle—I didn't have enough money to buy a car— my dad supported it. He even put up half the money I needed to buy it, so we were co-owners. I was the only kid in Hamburg with a motorcycle, and I loved roaring through town on it.

I didn't have my full license yet, only my permit, so I couldn't ride my bike at night—or at least, I wasn't supposed to. But my dad would ride it whenever he wanted. After a while, I started feeling resentful, like he was taking advantage of the situation. I started removing the license plate and hiding it when I wasn't riding so that my dad couldn't monopolize the bike. It started feeling like another strain, another competition, another conversation we weren't having.

We didn't do much together; sometimes we stayed up late playing backgammon for money. One night—a school night—we played until eleven or midnight before going to bed. Just as I was about to fall asleep, my body twitched: the involuntary muscle spasm people have as they drift off. At that moment, I heard a woman's shrill scream pierce the night, long and anguished.

I sat up with a start and ran to my dad's room. "Dad! Dad! Did you hear that?"

"Hear what? What's going on?"

"I heard a scream."

"Nobody screamed."

I went back to my room and grabbed the pool cue I kept by the side of my bed, thinking I could use it as a club. I ran outside. I roamed throughout the complex, looking behind dumpsters, listening for another scream. It was peaceful and quiet, no one else outside.

I went back inside and went to sleep.

At school the next day, I was called to the office. As I walked through the halls, my mind raced as I tried to think of what prank or misdeed I was going to have to explain away. Instead, I opened the door to see Lisa, her face crumpled, her eyes red with tears. She told me the news: my fourteen-year-old cousin, Tommy, had been drinking at a party the previous night, and on his way home he'd tripped while crossing a creek, passed out, and drowned.

I couldn't believe it. My cousin, who was just a kid?

I was sad, of course, and I was overcome with grief at his funeral.

What was that scream I heard the night my cousin drowned? Before anybody knew that he was dead? I believe that what I heard was something no one else in the apartment complex did. I have my private ideas about what it was, but I'll never really know.

My cousin's senseless accident is just one of many moments I will never understand. Considering the drunken, idiotic chances I took, why did nothing like that ever happen to me?

. . .

I'd been dating a girl named Wendy, my first real girlfriend, who I'd met at S.P.I.T. I'd convinced myself we were in love, but after three months she was starting to distance herself from me—not answering my calls, not meeting with me. I was a wreck about it. One night I hitchhiked the two-hour trip to her house, but she seemed distracted. She wouldn't sit still, didn't hold my hand. A few weeks earlier, I had slept in her mom's car in their apartment complex driveway so that I could see her bright and early the next day. I planned on doing it again and told her I'd see her in the morning. But this time she said I should go home.

So I started hitchhiking the long way back home, feeling like shit. One guy dropped me midway home, but after that no one stopped, and once it was ten p.m., I realized I wouldn't make it home. I called Dad collect from a payphone and explained my predicament.

"Get home," he said.

"But Dad, I can't," I protested. "I can't get a ride."

"Just get home. I don't care how you do it."

God, that pissed me off. I knew Dad was trying to teach me life lessons, like when he sat me at the kitchen table and had me smoke a cigarette and drink whiskey. But it was the middle of the night and I was still an hour from home. I called Mom, and she and Lisa came to get me right away.

I was at an awkward age—sixteen going on fifty. I felt independent and wanted to be treated as an adult, but I also wanted to have a safety net. It's kind of like a kid learning to ride a bike without training wheels; he doesn't want his parents holding onto the seat, but he wants them around if he's about to fall.

After that incident, I decided to move back in with my mom, taking her up on her promise that I could come back any time, no questions asked. I wasn't happy about living with her again, but at least I knew that at her house, I had pretty much free rein; sure, she had more rules, but I believed I could always outsmart her. More than ever, I just tried to avoid my parents.

This usually meant spending time with Cindy, my next girlfriend. We made an odd couple. Cindy was exceptionally smart; she ended up being the valedictorian of the class below me, destined for the Ivy League. I was failing out of school. But she wasn't just smart in a bookish way. She was also witty, and I loved being around her and her family—her dad played in a band and had a hearse he drove to gigs. My mom really liked Cindy, too, so she had no problem leaving us together unsupervised.

Meanwhile, Cindy's best friend Carrie was

off-and-on dating a guy named Jim, a stereotypical dumb jock football player. Cindy and Carrie came to the house a lot, and eventually Carrie got interested in Billy, who was always around me because we did things together. Billy was younger, yes—but girls loved him. He was charismatic, attractive, and a rising football star. So it was often the four of us: me and Cindy, and Billy and Carrie.

One night when we were all at Carrie's house, we heard someone banging on the door.

"It's Jim," Carrie gasped. "Billy, go hide."

We all knew how angry and violent Jim could be; he always seemed to be starting fights, whether on the field, in school hallways, or convenience store parking lots. Billy dashed into the bathroom and climbed into the bathtub, staying there while Jim yelled and cursed at Carrie, the rest of us holding our breath. Jim may have been a good football player, but he seemed to have no footing off the field. His insecurity and jealousy were frightening. Finally he left, slamming the door behind him.

Later that night I told Cindy, "Carrie's playing games with Jim."

She nodded reluctantly.

"You should stop her," I went on. "If he does something to hurt Carrie and you haven't tried to stop it, you'll be partly to blame."

"I know, I know," Cindy said with a sigh. "I should say something."

It's an ironic memory to reflect on, a painful memory. Cindy never said anything—but she wasn't the only one who could have changed how things turned out. After all, Carrie wasn't the one who ended up getting hurt.

. . .

Soon after that, Carrie's parents were going out of town, and we made plans to spend the night at her place. Mom drove us there even though she knew Carrie's parents weren't going to be around. It seemed an un-Mom attitude even then—she had so many rules for us—but maybe she was relieved to have us out of the house so she could go to the Golden Nugget without having to worry about us.

It was a low-key, uneventful evening. We drank a little bit, and then we went to sleep, Billy in bed with Carrie and me in another room in bed with Cindy.

In the middle of the night, Carrie was awakened by the beam of a flashlight coming through her bedroom window. She screamed, waking the rest of us. "There's someone outside! Oh God!"

And then—a hard crash at the front door, the tinkling sound of falling glass. Cindy and I rushed over and stood in horror, watching as Jim reached through the pane he'd punched through, his hand a bloody mess, and unlocked the door.

He came inside, his face twisted with anger. He wore red running shorts and untied brown work boots, but no shirt. He steamed into Carrie's bedroom and started attacking Billy. He hit him without stopping, full of rage. It felt like a dream; I'd never seen someone so angry.

I rushed over and wrenched Jim away from my

brother. "You just need to leave now," I shouted.

And he did. He stomped away, a trail of blood dripping from his hand.

Billy was shaking, and I grabbed his shoulder. "It's okay," I told him. "Everything's okay, he's gone."

But he wasn't gone. He'd only left to get his gun.

I didn't see it at first, when he came back into the room. He had it concealed behind his thigh. Again and again I've replayed the film in my head—if only I had seen the gun.

Carrie was screaming. Cindy had her hand over her mouth.

Jim kicked Billy. "I can't believe you fucked her!" he screamed.

Billy tried to push Jim away from him, and then I heard two shots: *pop! pop!*

In a blur, Jim grabbed Carrie, threw her over his shoulder, and ran.

He shot Billy.

"Did he hit you?" I asked, rushing over.

Billy, dazed, patted at his upper arm. One of the shots had hit his arm and gone into his chest.

I wrapped my arms around him and held him. "It's going to be okay," I said. "It was just a pellet gun."

The shots sounded soft—it couldn't have been a real gun—he shot my brother—no way it was a real gun.

"No," Billy said. "I felt gunpowder."

The police came, along with an ambulance. The paramedics put Billy on a gurney and rushed him off to the hospital. I wanted to go with him, but the police had questions for me.

As I watched, one officer took his pen, bent to the floor, and lifted a shell casing from the carpet. It hadn't been a pellet gun.

I looked down at my shaking hands. They were covered in my brother's blood.

Chapter 3

Against the Wind

It took a moment for my eyes to adjust to the darkness of the hospital room; the only light shone dimly from beneath a corner work station. I heard a low hum and sharp beeps from the machines monitoring Billy's vital signs.

My brother was asleep under the crisp, bleached-white covers, a tube in his chest. The bullet had entered his upper right arm and passed through his lung, collapsing it, before lodging near his spine. Though he would never be able to play football again—the bullet could move and paralyze him—he was going to be okay.

I should be the one in that bed, I should have taken that bullet, I thought as I watched my little brother lying there. *I should have stopped Jim, should have done something—anything—to protect Billy.*

I heard that the police had captured Jim—they'd

found him hiding in the cemetery, after he'd released Carrie, who was shaken but physically unharmed— and he was being held in jail, waiting to be charged. A friend of mine told me that suicidal prisoners were confined, strapped to their beds to keep them from harming themselves, so I called the jail and said Jim was suicidal. If Billy was going to be stuck in bed with a tube in his chest, Jim was going to be stuck in bed with straps around his ankles and wrists. *Screw the bastard. He deserves it.* I was furious.

As far as I was concerned, Jim had attempted to murder Billy. But he was allowed to plead to the lesser charge of reckless endangerment, basically claiming an accident had happened because of carelessness—like if I pulled out a gun at a party to show people and it somehow went off and hit someone in the leg. This guy had assaulted Billy, left, and come back with a gun. It wasn't an accident.

When we heard rumors that Jim would get only a slap on the wrist, I wrote a letter to the judge: "It's reassuring to know that if I don't like somebody, I can shoot him and not get punished." Jim ended up being put on probation and had to spend his weekends in jail for a few years.

And I couldn't avoid him. I'd blown off school and gotten bad grades, so I had to go to summer school before my senior year. So did Jim. He sat two seats back and to my left. I just had to sit there, trying to focus on schoolwork, with the person who shot my brother ten feet away from me.

I was terrified. I felt a kind of fear I'd never felt

before—fear that something horrible could happen again, fear about how vulnerable I was, fear that everything I had could be taken from me in a second.

Who was looking out for me?

My mom had been the one to agree to lesser charges for Jim. She told me it was not because she wanted him to get off easy, but so that she could sue Jim's family's homeowners insurance. The homeowner's policy would be responsible if the incident was the result of something reckless, like a gun going off in the air, but not for an attempted murder. The insurance paid out $100,000; the lawyers got a third, my mom and I got $3,000 each for emotional pain and suffering, and Billy got the rest. It's true I wanted the $3,000 because I wanted to buy a car—but I didn't understand how much it would affect me to see my brother's attacker walk away like nothing had happened.

It was brutal to see him in summer school, feeling his eyes on the back of my head. Or at least it felt that way to me. I have no idea whether he stared at me. Most probably he felt as threatened by me as I did by him. At that time, though, I felt fear; I worried I was next on Jim's list.

I don't know how the school system allowed that to happen. More importantly, I don't know how my parents allowed that to happen. They *knew* the fucker who shot Billy was in my class, and they didn't do a damn thing about it. What were they thinking? How could they not try to protect me?

I felt abandoned and afraid, but I wasn't going to feel defenseless ever again.

It's easier to see the beginnings of things than the ends—or maybe things just start more easily than they stop. Even then I knew I was entering a new era. Things were different. I was different. Everything was changing.

I'd always loved going through my katas, meditative sequences of martial arts moves. I was drawn to the peace, love, hug-a-tree philosophy of martial arts. Now I wanted nothing to do with that. I wanted full-on, full-body, no-holds-barred fighting. I was *pissed.*

I filled an old mailbag with sand to use as a punching bag and hung it in the garage, attacking it until my knuckles bled and the tops of my feet were scratched and bruised. I started fighting differently, hitting the bag differently. And I didn't confine my aggression to the gym. I never ran my mouth, but if someone started chirping at me, it was on. *You want some of this, fucker? Let's go.*

I settled arguments, even small ones, with my fists. I started carrying weapons. One night at the Inferno teen nightclub, I got into an altercation on the dance floor and pulled a butterfly knife on the guy. Out of nowhere a short, stocky guy with close-cropped hair approached me. "I'm a Green Beret," he said. "You better put that knife away." Why a Green Beret was at a teen club, I have no idea. But to this day I think he was a guardian angel. *Put that knife away. Why are you trying to ruin your life?*

If that was a wake-up call, I didn't hear it—I stayed reckless, angry. One night, as I headed into Inferno, the bouncers frisked me and confiscated a knife. A different night, I was having some problems with a couple of big guys, so I went out to the car and got my nunchucks. I put them under my jacket, took them into the bathroom, and was warming up when a bouncer came in and confiscated them.

I was beyond giving a shit. I didn't go out of my way looking to make trouble, but if it came my way, I was going to be ready. I wasn't going to run away from it, and I certainly wasn't going to stand there and watch it the way I watched Jim—I was going to fight back. And when I did feel fear rising up, it made me fight back harder than ever.

One summer night at the Erie County Fair, just before the start of my senior year in high school, some friends of mine and I hopped the fence and were walking around when two guys—one muscular, one fat, both big—tried to start a fight with me.

"Hey, Bielinski!" they called. "Hey pussy!"

I didn't even know who these guys were, and I had no idea how they knew my name. Maybe my reputation as the guy who did karate demonstrations had spread beyond my school. *Whatever*, I thought. *I don't need to fight you.* I ducked around the corner and rejoined my friends, who'd stepped over to the ringtoss booth. The bullies had caught me off guard, and they were big. I was scared.

At home that night, I felt terrible. Those guys had called me a pussy, and I felt like one. I decided to go back to the fair the next day. If I saw them, I'd fight them.

Sure enough, they found me. "There's the pussy

Bielinski," the muscular guy taunted. *Who the hell are these guys?* They were trying to start something with me, and on top of that, they were doing it while I was with my friends.

"Okay," I said. "We're going to fight—now."

They nodded in the direction of a nearby barn. We'd fight behind it, to avoid security guards. They walked in front of me, shoulder to shoulder, hatching a plan. My only plan was to try to keep both of them in front of me. The last thing I wanted was for one of them to wrap me up from behind while the other one beat the shit out of me.

As we got behind the barn, spectators were already gathering, a whisper running through the crowd: "Bielinski's going to fight."

The muscular guy, who I later learned was named Jack Fry, removed his shirt. His physique was no joke, and I knew I'd have my hands full with this guy, let alone him *and* his fat friend—whose name I learned was Ron Kemp. I removed my shirt, too, and instinctively threw some practice kicks into the air.

"Bielinski, I'm going to shove that karate up your ass," Fry said.

We started circling each other, looking for an opening, when I realized I'd lost track of Kemp. *Oh, shit. I'm going to get my ass beat here.* All I could do now was remain focused on Fry and hope I wasn't ambushed. I heard a rustling behind me—Kemp was making his move.

One of my friends, a small kid named Rob, jumped in front of him. Rob was no fighter, but he was an Eagle Scout—I guess he felt some sense of duty to protect my six. Somehow, Rob distracted Kemp or drew him into the circle of spectators, and now it was just me and Fry. He tackled me, and we both hit the ground, but I was back on my feet in an instant. As he rose, I kicked him in the stomach, struck him in the face, and then head-butted him. He dropped to the ground as a gasp rose from the crowd, covering his face and waving in surrender.

"Okay," I said. "Where's the fat fuck? He wanted some, too."

I strained to find Kemp, standing on my toes to get a 360-degree view of the crowd circling us, ten people deep. I never found him, but I did catch a glimpse of the security guards as they made their way over. Fry was still on the ground, bloodied, with a welt the size of an orange forming over his left eye. I got kicked out of the fair.

It was a small price to pay for the boost to my reputation. Fry and Kemp, I discovered, were well-known bullies from a rival school who beat up kids all the time. Now the word was out: Bielinski just beat the shit out of Fry. Everyone heard about it. Soon after that, when someone got in my face about something, his friend would pull him back: "That's John *Bielinski*," he'd hiss. The guy would back off quickly. No one was bothering me anymore.

My toughness and my reputation didn't help me in class or during those long nights when I couldn't sleep, worried about the parts of my life I couldn't control. The big house in Hamburg grew colder and emptier as my mom sold off furniture to make ends meet. Eventually she moved with me and Billy into a trailer—Lisa was gone now, off having her own adventures. It was a luxury trailer, but we were still moving from the most impressive house in Hamburg into a trailer. It felt like Mom had just erased the first sixteen years of my life. Nothing was familiar, nothing felt right. My own home was strange to me now.

Meanwhile, I was failing out of high school. There was no way I would graduate—at least not on time, not with my attitude. Instead of making me ashamed, this annoyed me. What options did I have for building a life? What job prospects did I have? I wasn't even thinking about college, given how much I hated school. I didn't have many options, but one stood out as the clear choice. In my mind I'd become a badass, and the idea of joining the US Marines—the most badass fighting organization ever known—made more sense than anything else. I was a fighter, and fighting would be my future. I didn't end up graduating from high school because I couldn't pass the state math exam. In the end, I believe I set a state record by failing it five times. And then I enlisted—the Marines would allow me to get my GED later.

A lot of people ask whether the Marines attract Marines, or whether the Marines make Marines. I believe people are attracted to the Marines because they've got that edge to them—that pit bull fighter mentality.

But having that edge didn't stop me from being uncertain and even afraid. As I waited for my enlistment to begin, I wondered whether I had what it took to be a Marine. I may have been tough in Hamburg, but I had no idea if I was tough enough for the world's most elite fighting force. I worried I'd be a failure as a Marine, just as I had been as a student.

I knew one thing, though: there was nothing in Hamburg to keep me there.

So I counted down the days until I would head to Marine Corps Recruit Depot Parris Island in South Carolina. The night before I was set to leave, I sat in the trailer chatting with my mom and Cindy. Although Cindy and I had drifted apart after Billy got shot, and I'd dated other girls during senior year, she was a regular visitor to the trailer. Sometimes I thought Mom liked Cindy more than she liked me.

The recruiters would be there soon to take me to a motel by the airport; they probably used this strategy to cut down on the number of guys who changed their minds about going. In the morning I'd fly to South Carolina and take a bus with other recruits to Parris Island.

I found my camera and took off my shirt. "Take a 'before' picture," I said to my mom, flexing my arms. I was sure that at boot camp, I'd undergo a transformation.

Soon two Marine recruiters rapped on the door. I said my brief goodbyes with Mom and Cindy and followed the recruiters to their car.

I'll never forget that drive to the airport motel. With each passing second, each shadowed building and tree, I was leaving behind the only world I really knew, shattered though it was—my family, my friends, the roller rink, Inferno. I was heading into a dark unknown. As we drove under flickering streetlights, past the houses and schools I'd attended, I suddenly felt a wave of grief. Shielding my eyes with my right hand, curling my lips and mashing them hard, I cried silently. I was scared.

I pulled myself together when Dad came to the motel to say goodbye. It wasn't in him to say he was proud or that he loved me, so he shook my hand, handed me a hundred-dollar bill, and left me alone with my fear.

The next day I learned I wasn't alone. Riding the white Marine Corps bus from the airport to Parris Island, I noticed the other recruits were quiet, the smell of stinking nervous sweat thick in the air. We had thought of ourselves as tough guys in our hometowns, but now we were about to find out.

I felt my chest knot as we drove onto the base and passed the entrance sign: "WELCOME TO PARRIS ISLAND: WE MAKE MARINES." My mouth was dry, my palms damp.

The bus pulled to a stop and a drill instructor came aboard. In a quiet, hoarse voice, he said, "Okay, guys. All hell is about to break loose for you. Follow instructions. Do what you're supposed to do." With that, he turned and left.

He was instantly replaced by another drill instructor, this one much louder. He barked, "Get off the bus and onto the yellow footprints!" he yelled. "Move it, girls! Let's go!"

It was going to be a long twelve weeks.

We scrambled off the bus as quickly as we could, stumbling our way onto the pavement and toward a bunch of spray-painted yellow footprints. Then the yelling *really* started.

The first few days were scary and confusing.

Ridiculously imposing men wearing Smokey the Bear hats yelled at us constantly, getting so close to our faces that the brims of their hats jabbed our noses and foreheads. Our job was to keep from getting yelled at. Their job was to break us, strip us of our individuality, and remake us into blindly obedient Marines.

I resisted.

During the first couple of weeks, we were mostly getting processed and learning how to be Marines. This meant paperwork, orientations, and medical checks. I was in a medical receiving line when I heard people in front of me moaning and groaning. We were supposed to stand rigidly in line, but once I got a few people away from where the recruits were moaning, I leaned over to the left to see what was going on.

I saw one recruit drop his pants, and a nurse next to him held up a large-bore needle and gave him a shot in the ass. It looked like a four-inch needle, and I could just imagine it going right into bone. I'd never liked needles; in high school, I'd given blood and passed out. When I saw what was going on, I thought, *Oh, fuck. Shit, I can't pass out in front of everybody.*

A memory flashed into my head. When I was nine years old or so, I had the revelation that if I snuck into my mom's room while she was sleeping, tiptoeing carefully, she'd wake up every time. Her subconscious got suspicious, and that would stir her. If I walked in there boldly, though, without thinking about it, she kept right on sleeping.

Standing in the receiving line, I took a deep breath, turned quickly, and walked out of line as if I'd been

ordered to. Getting out of line was unimaginable,
but I walked with so much authority that nobody
noticed. I simply skipped the nurse and joined the line
of recruits rubbing their butts after getting the shot.
I started rubbing my butt, too.

I didn't get caught that time, but usually I found
myself in plenty of trouble. I talked at the wrong time,
made the mistake of looking drill instructors in the
eye, didn't move quickly enough. One time, we were
going to go on a march and had to pack a duffle bag
to hold our things. My things didn't fit, so I asked
Drill Instructor Sergeant Bates whether I could use a
different bag. "Bielinski, you're nothing but a spoiled
doctor's kid!" he shouted, his spittle coating my face.

Drill Instructor Sergeant Bates was a mean
motherfucker who made our lives miserable. Short and
muscular—a wiry body built for leverage. Rotten teeth
from the chewing tobacco he always had in his mouth.
A tattoo on his left forearm reading, "Against the Wind,"
which I always wondered about until he explained
it one day: "My strategy of training Marines is like a
kite," he said. "The more wind you push on the kite, the
higher it'll go." No one could say he didn't push us. One
time he ordered everyone in the platoon to put their
shower shoes, running shoes, and boots in a pile in
the middle of the barracks. He planted a Marine flag
in the pile and then told us to find our shoes. He called
it Mount Suribachi—the mountain where the famous
photograph of Marines raising the flag at Iwo Jima was
taken. He was a real dick.

I was always in trouble, so I developed a reputation.

My punishment was extra calisthenics on the quarterdeck. "Bielinski, get on my quarterdeck." Every day I'd hear my name called, even when I hadn't done anything wrong.

But for about an hour each Sunday, I found some relief in church. I even volunteered to be a Catholic lay reader. I'd never really connected with the Catholic faith; even as a kid, I thought Catholicism was more about following rules than it was about God. But I enjoyed going to Mass on Sundays during boot camp. It was an hour that was a little less intense. As I trained to be a lay reader, though, I found myself again butting heads—this time with the priest.

He was training us to be able to be Eucharistic ministers on the battlefield, serving Communion to other soldiers. He held up the Communion wafer, a hard little disc of bread. "This," he said, "is Jesus's body."

I raised my hand. "But not really," I said. "Right? It's bread. It's a metaphor."

"Recruit Bielinski, once the host is consecrated, it's the body of Christ," he said, "and if you keep questioning, you'll be guilty of blasphemy." That was it— end of story, no explanation about Catholic doctrine, no discussion. Whatever the priest said was law. That was exactly the wrong approach to take with me. I wanted to understand why we were doing things a certain way. I didn't want to be a blind follower.

But boot camp had been designed to wear down people just like me—stubborn, individualistic, full of ego—and turn us into Marines. Drill Instructor Sergeant Bates may have been a dick, but he was a dick who made boys into Marines. Doing the same thing day in and day out, shouting, "Sir yes sir! Sir no sir!" along with the chorus of voices, marching and cleaning and practicing and fighting—I started feeling like I was part of something far bigger than myself. I felt myself becoming part of a group—the proud, the few: US Marines.

I started to feel the thing that had drawn me to the Marines in the first place: this was a badass group, and I wanted to be one part of this well-oiled machine.

I started liking parts of boot camp, especially competitions with other platoons. I was unstoppable on the obstacle course, and I was a monster with pugil sticks, which are designed to teach bayonet and close-combat fighting. I got so good with them that I would be assigned two opponents at once, and I'd still win.

We also had classes, and I discovered what it felt like to actually enjoy learning. Unlike in high school, where I could never see how algebra would ever help me, I found myself riveted: I was learning things like compass navigation so I could take a firing squad through a hot zone. Even the lessons in Marine Corps history appealed to me, because they felt like stories I could learn from.

I was now in my element. When I took the required Armed Services Vocational Aptitude Battery—a test to determine our post-training placement—I aced it. My scores qualified me for special anti-terrorism duty at key facilities. Once I completed boot camp and infantry school, I would be assigned to an anti-terrorist security post for my first two years of duty. I had gotten off to a rocky start in boot camp, but I had emerged a confident and capable Marine.

After boot camp I took a quick trip home on leave. A funny thing happened one day as I was driving down the street. I was stunned to see a beautiful blond girl walking on the sidewalk. I was surprised I had never seen her before—I thought I knew everyone in town. I assumed she must be new. As I drove slowly past and ogled her shining hair and long legs, I had the shocking realization that it was Tina Jones—my old best friend Bobby's little sister. She had clearly grown up, and I made a point to visit Bobby while I was home so I could get a closer look at her. They were both in town for a brief visit with their father. I tried to play it cool, but I was drawn to her. I returned to the Marines.

I shipped out for Camp Pendleton in California for infantry school, the second phase of training. Here we'd learn to fire the M47 Dragon, the dragon missile, to take down tanks and armored personnel carriers, and we'd also learn tactics and complete rigorous physical training. Our two months at Camp Pendleton would culminate in us strapping on combat loads—sixty-pound packs—and humping up "Mount Motherfucker." I'm sure that wasn't the mountain's real name, but after marching it once, that's what everyone called it.

While I was at Camp Pendleton, I again made plans to meet up with Bobby Jones. While his dad still lived in Hamburg, his mom had moved with the kids to Irvine just a few months after the divorce. They were now just an hour from where I was. I was eager to see Tina again after briefly connecting with her back home. I took the bus to their house, staring out the windows at the palm trees whipping past.

Standing on the doorstep, I was nervous. Would the Jones family even want to see me? Would I only be reminding them of an era they would prefer to forget? When Mrs. Jones—Cindy—opened the door, though, she greeted me with a warm hug.

When she moved aside, my jaw dropped to see Tina once again. Tina was almost eighteen years old, and she was the most beautiful girl I'd ever seen. More beautiful than when I saw her in Buffalo. I realized that I was staring: at her long blonde hair, tanned limbs, and deep brown eyes, my eyes following her curves. I stammered and tried to act casual until Bob came and rescued me.

We went down to Tijuana, crossing the border and hopping into a Mexican cab that was like a carnival ride, the driver cornering as if the car was on rails. Twenty bucks would last us the whole day, buying us all the bacon-wrapped hotdogs and tequila we wanted. Casually, I asked about Tina. "She's dating this dude—" Bob said with a sneer, "who has her name on his *truck*." I laughed, and Bob changed the subject, but I kept on thinking about Tina.

I went to visit Bob a few more times while I was at Camp Pendleton. I didn't really want to hang out with Bob, though—I wanted to spend time with his sister. I tried to extend my conversations with Tina; I tried to convince Bob to let her come surfing with us; I flirted wildly with her and tried to make her laugh. I discovered that not only was she beautiful, she was smart and sharp, making me laugh and calling me on my bullshit. I was pretty sure we had chemistry, but she had a boyfriend, and a very possessive boyfriend at that—what could I do?

Then, on my last day of infantry school, Tina came to see me on base. I rounded a corner and there she was, her summery dress flapping against her legs in the breeze. When she saw me, her face broke into a broad smile. In that moment, I wasn't thinking about her boyfriend, or our parents' complicated history, or the future. I wasn't thinking at all. I just scooped her into one arm, lifted her up, and kissed her. We said goodbye, but we both knew it wasn't forever.

After a couple of weeks at security forces school—which I spent mostly at a firing range, learning to shoot bad guys and avoid good guys—I went back to Buffalo for a month of recruiting duty before I began my security detail post. Tina was there, too, visiting her dad, and I was staying with my mom. Tina's boyfriend wasn't in the picture anymore.

We started seeing each other, and I fell for her hard and fast. We spent all our free time together—at my mom's place, at her dad's house, sometimes just going on drives. I took her out on my motorcycle, racing along back streets littered with leaves, basking in the glow I felt with her arms around my waist. I'd never felt like this about a girl before.

My mom hated that I was dating Tina Jones. Of course she did—this was the daughter of the woman who had been her best friend before sleeping with her husband, tearing apart both their marriages. We never had a long conversation about it, but she would make sarcastic comments or roll her eyes if I said something about Tina.

"Is that *girl* coming for dinner?"

"I'm not dating *Cindy*," I said.

"That's enough," Mom said with a warning glare.

It must have been so difficult for my mother—so painful, so embarrassing—but the more she protested and disapproved, the more strongly I was drawn to Tina.

In late 1988, eight months into my time with the Marines, I was assigned to Norfolk, Virginia, as part of an anti-terrorist unit at NATO headquarters. When I said goodbye to Tina, I handed her a letter. I had written and rewritten it about fifteen times, trying to get it just right. "Don't read it until I'm gone," I said. In the letter, I told Tina how strong my feelings for her were. I knew we were going to be apart for a long time and far away from each other, but I didn't want to lose her.

She felt the same way. Once I was in Norfolk, we wrote and talked constantly. I told her about my new job working the gate at NATO headquarters, checking IDs. I described the club we Marines sometimes went to and the beach where we played volleyball. I told her about how I was getting back into full-contact martial arts, training with a black belt at a local gym. I even told her how my big sister, Lisa, had settled in Norfolk after a series of adventures that included being employed by a carnival that crisscrossed the country for months at a time.

Meanwhile, I signed up to fight in the National Armed Forces tournament. I was used to tournament fighting, but I figured full-contact fighting couldn't be much different, so I signed up for the advanced bracket. After all, it was open to brown belts and up, and I was a brown belt.

But I didn't realize how good my opponents would be. I fought in two matches against guys as flexible as ballerinas; the second one was strong enough to kick me clear out of the ring. They called both matches and insisted I go down a level to intermediate, where I won every fight. At one tournament, a grandmaster approached me and shook my hand. "I saw those fights you did at the advanced level," he said, looking at me with interest. "You wouldn't quit. We were very impressed." I told Tina about this, of course, bragging over the phone line as I lay on my back in my bunk, staring up at the ceiling, picturing her, hoping she would be impressed, too.

Despite being on opposite sides of the country, Tina and I got more and more serious. We joked about how complicated our relationship was, quoting the old line: "Oh, what a tangled web we weave." I told Tina, "Someday I'm going to get a boat and name it *Tangled Webs.*"

Tina made a decision—she was going to transfer schools and come live with her dad in Buffalo. I was thrilled. This meant I could see her a once a month. I started coming home whenever I could, either hopping a flight or driving the eight hours. I even lied to my commanding officer, saying I had a family emergency and had to go home.

I had never told a girl I loved her before, but I felt that way about Tina and wanted to say those scary, wonderful words to her. One night as we lay in bed, staring into each other's eyes, I took a deep breath—but Tina was faster than me. "I love you," she said with a smile. I laughed and wrapped her up in a hug, singing the Meat Loaf lyrics that came into my head: "Well you took the words right out of my mouth."

In November 1989, Tina came to Norfolk to be my date for the Marine Corps Ball. It was a magical night, with off-the-charts pageantry, all of us Marines in our crisp dress blues with swords, medals, and ribbons. Tina and I held hands and walked out onto the floor for the first slow dance of the night. She looked breathtakingly beautiful in her sweeping white gown, her blonde hair shimmering under the lights. "Way to go, Bielinski!" my commanding officer shouted.

Falling asleep with Tina in my arms that night, I felt like my life was finally going in the direction I wanted. I was doing well in the Marines, I was disciplined, and I was so in love with Tina that I would have gone through a brick wall for her. I could finally look at the future and see something clear and good.

A few weeks later, Tina called. Her voice was uncharacteristically high and agitated. "We need to talk," she said.

I felt my stomach churn. *Is that California guy back in the picture? Is she sick?* "What's wrong?"

In the silence that followed, I heard a muffled sob. Then: "I'm pregnant."

Chapter 4

Operation Inner Storm

Pregnant? It can't be. She's on the pill.

"What's really going on?" I asked.

"What do you mean? *We* had sex and *I* got pregnant."

"How can you be sure?"

"John," Tina said, "I'm sure." She had gone to Planned Parenthood, she said—she'd gotten a blood test.

She couldn't be pregnant. I didn't believe her. I even called up Planned Parenthood to find out how they did pregnancy tests, looking for a way out, looking for evidence that what Tina said wasn't true.

And then the whisper campaign started. Never one to keep secrets, I told my friends and family what was going on. Lisa said she wanted to be supportive, and she wanted what was best for me. She also said she'd seen Tina with another guy. Some of my buddies from home said the same. Tina was being sneaky. Tina wasn't being honest.

My parents' reactions meant nothing to me at the time. I can't even remember what they said when I told them. Looking back, though, I know my mom must have felt overwhelmed: *Just when I thought it couldn't get any worse.*

Part of me believed that Tina was being deceptive. But I still loved her fiercely and would do anything for her. I knew I wasn't supposed to be glad about this news. After all, Tina and I weren't married, and I still had two years left in the Marines.

But over the next few weeks, I found myself growing eager and optimistic. I loved Tina, I loved kids, and I was going to be a dad—a *good* dad. I would teach my son or daughter important things; I would protect this child and prepare him or her for the world. I bought books on parenting and looked into buying an engagement ring. I wasn't just going to do the right thing—I was *excited* about doing the right thing.

But the more I embraced the idea, the more distant Tina became. When I called her, either she didn't pick up, or she was terse and formal. I tried to reassure myself: *Everything will make sense once we're together.* I was going to see Tina at Christmas. I dreaded the conflict and tension of my own family at Christmas— the hysterics my mom flew into when I left for my dad's house, the sterility and superficial conversation at my dad's—but I knew what Tina and I had was real. We were going to be fine.

But when she met me at the airport, I moved in to kiss her and she gave me her cheek. On the ride home, she seemed distracted until I brought up the baby.

"I'm reading this book on Lamaze," I said, breaking the silence.

"I haven't even decided whether I'm having the baby," Tina said sharply.

I tried not to sound panicked. The snowbanks lining the freeway flew past in a blur. "Isn't that something we should talk over together?"

"You're not the one who's pregnant."

I kept telling myself that things would be fine. She was hormonal and she was overwhelmed, just like I was, but we were meant to last. I was determined we *would* last.

But I dreaded facing her father, who already knew I had knocked up his daughter, making the tangled web of our families even messier. Still, if I was going to see Tina, I'd have to face her father sooner or later. So one day during my leave, I knocked at the door, heart racing. My hands were clammy despite the frigid weather. When Mr. Jones opened the door, I gulped.

"Johnny Bielinski!" he roared. "Get in here." He was smiling broadly, and once I'd entered the door he looked me over from head to toe before wrapping me in a hug.

"Sir, I have to be honest," I stammered once he'd released me. "I'm very uncomfortable right now."

He laughed. "Nobody's expecting you to marry Tina," he said. "As long as you support the baby, do your part financially, everything will be fine."

To my surprise, relief washed over me. I wasn't ready for marriage, and deep inside I must have known that.

But at the same time, I could feel anxiety spread through my stomach. *Is that all Tina wanted me for?*

I was ready to be a father—did she just want a paycheck?

For the rest of my time at home, Tina was a wall. She made excuses to avoid spending time with me, and even when she reluctantly agreed to see me, she was cold. One night as we drove to have dinner, I rubbed the back of her neck. She pulled away. Another night, I casually said, "Maybe if it's a boy, the baby could be named John."

"That's not going to happen," she said flatly.

Sitting in my car in her driveway, I watched her close the door, disappearing into the warm house. The pain I felt in that moment was so overpowering that I wished I'd never met her, had never seen her beautiful face.

It was clear that things were not okay—but everything was murky. Tina wasn't breaking up with me or cutting me out. But despite my many attempts, Tina was also unwilling to have a conversation with me about what was going on. Uncertainty swirled around us and around the baby. What was going to happen? What role would I play in this child's life? Back in Norfolk, I thought of Tina constantly. Obsessively. When I was training out in the field, away from the barracks for several days, my desperation to talk to her built in a wild crescendo. When I finally got her on the phone, she blew me off again. I felt like a tightly coiled spring.

All that mattered to me was numbing the pain. I turned to my usual method, my fists, trying to fight it all away. I fought at bars, I fought on the streets. I'd go to the gym, look for the biggest guy I could find, and challenge him to a boxing match. When I was home on leave, I would go up to Canada with Billy and get into brawls on dance floors. I would get off post and go punch the bag until my knuckles were bloody; I'd punch and punch and kick and kick, and when I couldn't kick anymore, I went back to punching. I never ran out of fuel.

One day I got pissed at my roommates, Seabresee and Phillips. Seabresee was a great guy; Phillips was a douchebag. But the three of us usually got along just fine. That day, I'd stood at the phone, dialing and redialing Tina's number for twenty minutes, listening to it ring, unanswered, in an increasing rage.

Just then, Phillips and Seabresee walked in. One of them—I don't even remember which—walked in and asked cheerfully, "Hey, man! Talked to Tina lately?"

"Fuck both of you," I said, slamming down the receiver. "I want you outside right now and I'm going to kick both your asses. I'll even bet twenty bucks a man I'll beat you both."

I knew I could drop Phillips, but Seabresee was a strong wrestler. I figured I'd attack him first. But I missed my aim and just grazed him with a kick. Seabresee picked me up and slammed me to the ground. Phillips made his charge as I was on my knees, but I was able to toss him aside. Just as I did, though, Seabresee nailed me in the temple. It was over.

I handed over twenty dollars to both of them, but Seabresee wouldn't take it. "I know you've got a lot of shit going on right now, but Jesus, Bielinski," he said. "You've got to calm the fuck down or you're going to get killed."

I didn't want to calm down. I wanted Tina back, or at least I wanted closure. I was sick of living in limbo.

Fighting wasn't enough—I starting drinking more, too. I often drove drunk. I wasn't thinking about the consequences at all. I was outside of myself, watching a grainy movie.

One night when I was on leave, I was driving home from Canada with Billy in the passenger seat. The night was still and peaceful, an inch or two of fresh snow blanketing the ground. We came to a red light. I looked up and down the cross street and didn't see a soul; I blew through the light. Moments later, flashing red lights swirled in my mirror. I pulled over, fumbling for my ID as the police officer focused a powerful flashlight beam through the side window glass.

"Just be cool and courteous," I murmured to Billy. "It's the guys who mouth off who get in trouble."

I rolled down the window. "You been drinking?" the officer asked.

"Yes, sir."

"Just get out of the car."

But when he saw my military ID, he softened. "You good to get home?" he asked. I nodded. "Be careful."

As I'd already done so often in my life, I wiggled out of trouble again. But instead of seeing the incident as a warning sign, I doubled down on drinking.

Back in Virginia, I went out drinking by myself one night and ended up so drunk that I went the wrong direction on a throughway, straight into oncoming traffic. I jerked the wheel hard, but I wasn't quick enough—I sideswiped a big black SUV. Two large men got out.

"Fuck you doing, man?" one asked. "You need to give us some money." It was a damp, chilly night, and mists rose up behind him. I couldn't see his face.

"I don't have any," I said. "I drank it."

The two men looked at each other, then jogged back to their car and drove off. Maybe they didn't want police involvement? I'll never know. Me, I walked unsteadily back to my car in the misty dark and drove back to the base. Yet again, I'd avoided serious trouble through sheer luck. But I was so lost in my confusion and pain about Tina, I didn't give my behavior a second thought.

I couldn't stop thinking about Tina. I couldn't stop fighting. I couldn't stop drinking. I was completely out of control. I even drank on duty once. I just left the base, went to a bar, and had drinks. Even while I was doing this, I knew how severe my punishment would be—I'd be finished, thrown in the brig and kicked out— but I couldn't help myself. I didn't care. And somehow, I didn't get caught.

Talking to my dad once, I confessed I was drinking too much. "Don't drink for a week," he said. "See how you feel."

That wasn't what I needed, in my opinion. I needed closure, I needed to heal, I needed to change the past. But whatever regrets I had, I failed to see how many more I could have had—how many times I'd been a hair's breadth from doing something I could never take back, something unforgivable.

An example: One weekend, Lisa hosted a cookout party for me and some friends at a park behind her house. We barbecued, drank beer, talked. Lisa had reserved the space, so the gate was locked.

But then a group of kids jumped the fence and caused a ruckus. One threw an apple at Lisa.

This was the ignition. I always was looking for the ignition. "What the hell are you doing?" I shouted, walking toward them. "You looking for trouble? You looking to scrap? You want some of this?" I felt my Marine buddies lining up behind me, a solid wall of muscle.

The kids scattered, but I knew they'd be back. I rushed into Lisa's house and found the gun she kept by her bed for protection, checked to make sure it was loaded, and put it into the waistband of my pants.

Sure enough, the group returned with their big brothers, who were carrying baseball bats and big sticks. One of the bigger guys walked over wielding a bat like a club. "What you gonna do?" he jeered.

"This," I said, pulling the gun from my pants.

Everyone gasped and backed away. "Crazy motherfucker has a gun," one of them said.

"He's got a twenty-five," exclaimed another.

He knows his guns, I thought.

As the kids scattered, Lisa whirled on me. "Jesus *Christ*, John, what the hell are you doing? Is that my gun?" She held out her hand, her face all disbelief and rage. "Do you understand you could have killed someone?!"

I shrugged and handed her the gun. I didn't care—a bunch of punk kids weren't going to mess with me and my family.

By the spring, I'd had months of uncertainty, fighting, drinking, fury, and pain. Then Tina called. I was home on leave—I can remember the scene in vivid detail. I was stretched out across my mom's rose-patterned bedspread, cradling the phone between my cheek and my shoulder, staring at the ceiling fan quietly spinning.

"We need to talk," Tina said.

What the fuck do we have to talk about? I thought. *I've been trying to talk for months.* "Okay," I said, a hint of irritation in my voice.

"I've been seeing my old boyfriend from California," she said. "He's living with me here in Buffalo."

I turned away from Lisa's teenage grin to face the blank wall on the other side. "That explains a lot," I said.

"He wants to marry me," she said, her voice cracking. "And he wants you to sign papers giving up your right to the baby."

I hadn't expected this. After months of yearning for closure, for certainty, here it was—and all I felt was numb. This was the decision Tina had made. This was the decision that made sense. This was a decision that would prevent us from being bound together, which had once been my greatest desire, but which now brought me nothing but pain.

"I want to meet him," I said gruffly.

"What?" she said. "No, I can just mail the papers to you."

I sat up on the bed. "I'm going to come over and meet him before I sign."

"Fine," she said. After a beat of silence, hesitation, she said: "But John, I don't want you starting—"

"I'll be nice," I said.

He was the one who opened the door, wearing a golf shirt and a forced smile. Tina stood behind him,

her lavender t-shirt stretched over her swollen belly.
I extended my hand, and he shook it firmly. We talked;
I can't remember what we said. He seemed decent.
"Okay," I eventually said. "Let's get these papers signed."

Holding the pen, I thought about everything this
would mean. I wouldn't see the baby. I wouldn't hold
the baby. I wouldn't teach him things. I wouldn't be
his dad. These thoughts felt far away, pushed down
into dark corners of my mind. I kept waiting to feel
waves of sadness, relief, anything at all—but instead the
numbness just expanded. I felt as blank and dense as if I
were made of chalk. I scrawled my name, the name this
child would not share after all.

And then, out of the numbness, one thread of
feeling arose: anger. *Fuck you, Tina.*

. . .

I kept pushing down my feelings about the baby, but
soon after I signed the papers, the fever broke. The days
still blended together and I still fought, but I felt less
desperate. The uncertainty with Tina and the baby had
weighed me down. Within a couple of weeks of signing
the papers, I felt lighter. At least I knew where I stood.
I had been wounded, but I would survive.

One day I was talking with a slim staff sergeant
who I saw at the gym a lot. I confessed I was getting
over a rough breakup.

"For a while there," I said, "I just didn't care about
anything."

"I saw that in you," he said. "But you still did your

job every day. As much as your life was in shambles, you still did your job, and that's what makes you a Marine."

. . .

Just as I was emerging from my haze, my tour at NATO headquarters was coming to an end. In summer 1990, I was reassigned to Camp Lejeune in Jacksonville, North Carolina, for two years of service with the fleet Marine force—essentially, the infantry. At Camp Lejeune, we'd train to be in combat readiness.

Halfway around the world, a situation was developing that would put our readiness to the test.

Under Saddam Hussein, Iraq had invaded Kuwait, taking more than one hundred American citizens captive. He later released them, but there was no way the United States was going to let something like that slide. As soon as I got to Lejeune, I began training in desert warfare—everything from keeping the Dragon Missile system operable in dusty conditions to extracting water from the desert.

A few months in, we went out on a battalion run—a couple hundred guys, led by a bigwig, running in formation. He ran us into a big field and called us into formation. We stood in perfect lines, the North Carolina humidity thick as molasses while the sun beat down.

"Platoon commanders, prepare your troops for deployment in Southwest Asia," he said. "Dis-missed!"

That was all: those were our orders to go overseas, to go into war. We were thrilled, buzzing with excitement. *Ooh-Rah!*

Once our unit and gear were in order, we were granted two weeks' leave to see family. I spent a lot of time with Billy, getting drunk and giving him hell for playing two women at once. At moments during these two weeks, the realization that I was going to war fell over me. This was really happening. People die in war, and I could be one of them.

I knew Tina had given birth to a baby boy; by now, he would be three months old. She—they—had named him Corey. When I thought about them, I pushed them from my mind. My family and friends didn't talk about them. It was easier not to think of what I was missing.

On my last night at home, Billy and I went out drinking with one of his girlfriends at a smoky dive pool hall. They had a huge blowup, yelling at each other in the bar.

"Let me take you back," I told her. "You and Billy can cool off." So Billy rode with someone else, and in my car, his girlfriend pumped me for information, screaming about how Billy was seeing someone else. She was right, but I wasn't about to betray my brother, so she got nothing out of me.

Billy was already home, sprawled on the couch with an open beer. I was about to tell him how his girlfriend was when she burst through the trailer door, screaming, "Johnny told me everything!"

I shook my head at this ploy. My brother trusted me.

But then—"You son of a bitch!" Billy yelled. "How could you stab me in the back like that?"

I stared at him in disbelief. How could this be happening? Billy kept yelling, spouting obscenities, his face twisted with rage. But I didn't fight back, even when he walked up and shoved me back onto the couch before storming out. In the silence that followed the slammed door, I just sat there in shock. This was *Billy*—how could he have been so angry at me? How could he not trust me?

The next day I sat at the airport, waiting to fly back to Camp Lejeune and then overseas. My mind was morning-after fuzzy and my heart was heavy. *I don't even know if I'm going to come home alive, and my last memory of my brother will be of him screaming at me.*

Then I heard someone yell, "Johnny!" It was Billy and my good buddy Trevor. They'd raced to the airport to see me before I left.

I don't even think Billy and I apologized to each other—we didn't have to. We wrapped each other in a huge bear hug. Trevor snapped a shot with a Polaroid and shook the little plastic square until the image appeared: brothers holding each other, hungover but grinning.

On December 15, 1990, I deployed to the Middle East. We landed under the cover of night. I remember stepping off the plane onto the tarmac, the air hot and thick with the acrid stench of jet fuel. *Shit just got real. We're in country now.*

Over the next two weeks, we acclimated ourselves in Tent City, getting used to the environment, the food supply, and the dechlorinated water. My calves ached every morning, sore from pushing off sand as I walked. We celebrated Christmas in the desert, and I broke out the small inflatable snowman I'd packed, putting us all in the Christmas spirit. I had also packed a radio, which made me very popular—we could listen to military programming.

We did physical training and tried to find ways of passing the time, waiting in the desert to fight. We played Dungeons & Dragons, which I'd loved as a kid. Other times we'd play God, intervening in the life-and-death struggles of the ferocious flies and ants that seemed to be everywhere. We pulled pranks.

At first we talked about girls. Then our conversations focused on food. Sometimes there was no hot chow in the chow line, but there was always a big vat of peanut butter. We were given only flimsy plastic utensils, but I kept in my pocket a sturdy metal spoon I'd stolen from the Camp Lejeune chow hall, perfect for scooping huge mounds of peanut butter and making sandwiches with a layer of peanut butter as thick as your thumb—just like Dad used to make. We talked for hours about pizza. Finally our conversations turned to beds and what we would do for a night on a real mattress.

Tensions ran high, stress and uncertainty building. Each day brought us closer to engaging with the enemy; every day brought us closer to the possibility of death. Marines got in fights and were threatened with the brig.

Nights I stared out into the vast desert sky, marveling at the stars. Sometimes you could read a book by the light of the moon and the stars, they were so bright. An arrow-shaped constellation pointed to exactly where we would be fighting.

I was overcome by a desire to see my son. Maybe it was all that thinking, all that pondering life and mortality—I was desperate to see his face, to see the person Tina and I had created. I wrote to Cindy Jones, Tina's mom. It was a long shot, but I asked her whether she could send some photos of Corey.

I hadn't been to church in months, but I made a deal with God. *If you let me see my son, I'll be prepared to die.* Days passed, each mail call a disappointment: nothing from Mrs. Jones.

But then, just when I'd given up hope—and as our unit positioned itself to drive into Kuwait—I got a thick envelope from Mrs. Jones.

We were bivouacked in a quarry as we prepared to mass for an attack. I ripped open the envelope and stared at the pictures—bright blonde hair, deep brown eyes, my son. As I stared at the photos, I could almost feel Corey's weight in my arms, his hot breath on my neck.

At that moment, I was full of indescribable joy and pain. After so much numbness, here was happiness flooding my heart, some part of me out there in the world, pure and good.

But now I knew beyond a doubt that I would die.

. . .

A few days later, the tension in our unit was as thick as the black smoke on the horizon before us. Although no one had said anything, we could tell we were about to go to war. The Iraqis knew it, too; the broiling smoke came from the oil field fires the Iraqis set before evacuating their forward positions. Each inhale brought a sharp, acrid stench into my nostrils. Each wind gust pelted us with gritty sand, and when the wind died down, flies swarmed our faces.

The commander gathered us around his tank.

"Men, tomorrow we'll be crossing the border of Kuwait," he said. "And the good news is, we're going to dominate. We will crush, and we will kick ass. We're Marines, and that's what Marines do."

"Ooh-Rah!" a Marine shouted in the spirit of an amen. I glanced around and saw proud smiles curling up on the faces of my fellow Marines.

The commander paused and looked in the direction of the shout, a look of deathly seriousness on his face. "The bad news," he said, "is that some of you are going to die tomorrow."

Shit is really getting real, I thought, swallowing hard, convinced I'd be among tomorrow's dead. *My mouth is dry. Why is it so damn dry?*

The commander continued: "Fight proud and with honor, Marines."

Get as many of those fucking ragheads as I can before they get me. Because they're going to get me—I know it.

The next day we rolled into Kuwait. I was in an armored vehicle, shoulder to shoulder with infantrymen. As we made our way into the uncertainty of combat, I thought about Billy. I imagined him at work or driving to school, overhearing a special bulletin on the radio: *After six weeks of aerial strikes, the US-led coalition forces launched a massive ground offensive today in Kuwait and Iraq. The military has not released casualty figures . . .* My heart ached as I pictured him not knowing. Would I ever get to talk to my brother again?

My stomach was churning with these thoughts when suddenly our vehicle lurched to a halt. The backdoor dropped and a sergeant popped out, dropped to a knee, and started shouting orders. The sound of live fire and explosions filled the air. Without warning, the sergeant dropped to the ground and started firing, really lighting it up downstream.

Fuck. What the fuck is this? Every Marine who leaped out of the vehicle started firing. *Oh shit. I don't want to get off this thing.* I don't know if I was ever more scared. I knew one thing: I didn't want to leave the relative safety of the armored vehicle.

Then came the order: "Dragons dismount! Dragons dismount!"

All of my training kicked in and I moved without thinking. My dragon team and I jumped out and got into the shit. There were three bunkers about one hundred yards in front of us and we were taking fire from their direction. I lit up the one on the far left. I loaded my M16 with tracer rounds to make sure my aim was true. I didn't know if the bunker I was firing on was empty or occupied, but I was sure as hell going to lay down effective suppressive fire.

Then over the sound of shouts and gunfire came a roar like rolling thunder as two Apache helicopters swooped down and hovered over the bunker, their big guns blazing. Something white popped up—a flag—then another, and another. Iraqis poured from the bunkers, all of them waving white flags of surrender.

I gritted my teeth in fury; I wanted the order to fire. The dragon missile was only supposed to be used against armor and bunkers, but I wanted to open up on those guys. *Fucking bastards. Why do you get to surrender? Raghead pricks deserve to die.* (Yeah—"raghead." Not proud. But that's the depersonalization of the enemy that comes with combat.)

Looking back, I am amazed at how desperately—full of anger, fear, and adrenaline—I wanted to kill.

On day three of the ground war, we halted outside of Kuwait City; our orders were to let the Kuwaitis take their city back themselves, for national pride. The halt allowed us to get out and look at the carnage along the road leading out of Kuwait City. We had engaged and destroyed the fleeing Iraqis. Dead bodies and body parts were everywhere. We saw guys burned to carbon, fingers still clutched around the steering wheels of decimated trucks.

The thing I remember most is how little this bothered me. I knew these had at one time been people, but I didn't feel any human connection with them. I'd been trained to dehumanize them in order to kill them if necessary. Walking amid the wreckage, I was mostly in awe of US firepower. Better them than me.

I didn't see any more direct action. As we continued our advance, we rarely got out of the armored vehicles—a precaution against shrapnel from exploding shells. We got out only to eat or form a perimeter. I still saw a lot that I'll never forget. I saw a wire-guided missile take out an enemy tank. I saw a donkey tied up in the desert with no one around, his legs bound by wire coat hangers. Another Marine and I cut him loose and watched him trot away over the vast swath of sand.

I didn't know then that this is how nomadic people keep their animals contained when there are no fences.

Although the war was over in a matter of days, it would take us months to get back home. We were so deep in Kuwait, and there were so many vehicles behind us, that making our way back proved more arduous than defeating the Iraqis.

I'd been so convinced that I would die that when my plane took off for home, I worried we'd be shot down somewhere over the Middle East. But hours later, when our plane touched down in North Carolina on April 15, 1991, I let out a sigh of relief. If I was going to die, I'd die on American soil.

I'll never forget the reception I got when I stepped off the plane in Buffalo. Friends and family, a sea of smiling faces, posters welcoming me back. My mom had handed out kazoos, and I was greeted by a hearty chorus of "When Johnny Comes Marching Home Again."

A couple of people asked me if I'd re-up, but that was never my plan. I used to say that I was on the "four years and sixteen seconds" program, because as soon as my four years were up, I figured it would take me sixteen seconds to get off the base. In fact, if I could have signed up for two years instead of four, I would have. I joined the Marines because I wasn't ready for college and wanted to tear things up a bit before I settled down. Sometimes now I regret not pursuing rank. But at the time, there was no question. The Marines Corp is a tough, hostile environment. You're always preparing for combat: no downtime, no relaxing—you are always being pushed, and as soon as you acclimate, they increase the pressure. I never considered staying on.

So while it was great to be home, now I had to readjust, reenter the world. Some things I had figured out already. I was going to live with Billy and my buddy Trevor, and I was going to attend Erie County Community College. I'd decided to study to be a landscape architect—this seemed like a good, solid plan.

But underneath this plan, I was full of doubts. Here I was, a burly Marine, a combat veteran no less, and yet I was *scared*—frightened by the prospect that I would fail at school. In the Marines, I'd been the smart guy, but I had no idea how I would do in college. What if I failed out, just like I had in high school? What if all my plans crumbled?

I was also haunted by the deal I'd made with God. It felt surreal that I was alive, and I felt a heaviness looming over me. God had delivered on His end of the bargain, showing me the face of my son, but I hadn't delivered on mine.

I felt there was a debt to be paid.

Chapter 5

Awakening the Giant

I was a Marine returning from a war that enjoyed broad support at home. People were in a patriotic mood, flying American flags and treating returning Marines with deference and respect. I was asked to speak at an elementary school. Every time I went out, people wanted to buy me a drink. People were treating me like a hero—but my life didn't exactly look like a hero's life.

A lot had changed during my time in the Marines: Mom had remarried to a guy named Jim; Dad had remarried to a woman named Agnes. Tina and her old boyfriend had moved with the baby to Wales, putting an ocean between us. Billy had started school at Erie Community College, where I planned to join him, living off what I'd saved as a Marine and with tuition covered by the GI Bill.

I moved in with Billy and Trevor as soon as I

returned in early January—just in time to start the spring semester. Trevor was a great friend of Billy's, and I'd met him when I was still in the Marines. He was a strong, good-looking guy who always attracted the attention of women. He was a lot of fun, and we had quickly become good friends.

We rented the ground floor of a two-story house, living below a young married couple and their kid. Our place was constantly trashed, pizza boxes with half-eaten crusts on end tables and piles of dirty dishes everywhere. Billy and I each had our own bedroom, and Trevor slept on the living room couch like a drifter. The dartboard in the living room served as the centerpiece of our social life. We instituted a lot of sensible rules— for example, we had a daily dart-throwing competition to determine who was Man of the Day, and if anybody farted audibly, he had to whistle immediately or everyone else could punch him until he did. We kept a swear jar and enforced it not just among ourselves, but also with visitors, even during parties. We got competitive about it—it was easy after a while to avoid dropping F-bombs, but those who visited our house seemed to find it quite difficult. That swear jar ended up funding a few well-deserved nights out. We had a volleyball net in the side yard, and given that our backyard was a cemetery, we didn't disturb our neighbors.

I needed a car to get around, and soon I found a white Volkswagen Rabbit, a crappy little car with a pathetic "meep meep" horn. I replaced it with a burly air horn, which—due to my substandard job of wiring the horn in place with a coat hanger—sometimes blared without being pushed.

At school, I felt awkward. Most of the other students were younger than me, fresh out of high school. Although at twenty-two years old I wasn't that much older, I felt out of place. I'd been to war; I'd fathered a son. The worst some of these kids had seen was the possibility of being turned down for a prom date. I was dog years older than these kids.

My professor for first-year English Composition had been Billy's teacher for the same class. "I've read about you," he told me. "For an assignment about the person who's been most influential in the student's life, your brother wrote about you."

I wondered what Billy could possibly have written. It seemed like a lot of the time I'd influenced him it was only to drink more booze. But I knew he was as proud of my service in the Marines as I was. A swell of pride ran through me, along with a resolve to set him a good example. But my resolve didn't last long.

I had always influenced Billy—and now Billy, Trevor, and I kept influencing each other, drinking and fighting. We went out drinking almost every night, and from the moment we walked into a bar, we owned it. The alcohol flowed; fists flew. Billy was never really a fighter, but when he was with me, he got beer muscles. Trevor was a strong guy and more than able to hold his own. The three of us combined were unstoppable.

We never went out intending to get into a fight, but again and again, somehow the fights found us. Maybe someone bumped into Billy and spilled some beer on him. *All right, let's go.* Maybe someone looked at us funny or called one of us pussies. The reason was never important. We were ready to get after it.

One night we were at a college bar, feeling no pain. Trevor had apparently had something going with one of the women in the bar, but now they were on the outs. She was hanging out with some frat guys, but Trevor tried talking to her to see if he could revive whatever it was they'd had.

Then, across the bar, illuminated in the rosy neon glow of a Genesee Beer sign, I saw two frat punks pinning Trevor up against the wall. "We already *told* you, stay the fuck away from her!" one of the guys yelled.

I glanced to the side and caught Billy's eye. He was already on it. We made it across the crowded room in a flash. I was about to launch myself at them when a bunch of guys grabbed me. I could see some other guys had Billy. I thrashed around wildly, trying to shake loose—but seeing the bouncers coming over, the frat boys let us go and moved toward the front of the bar.

Holy cow. There's like twenty frat boys here thinking they can manhandle us. I was revved up, my pulse hammering. "We've gotta get out of here or I'm going after those bastards," I told Billy.

We walked out holding our heads high—but then one of the little shits came after us and started running his mouth.

"Okay, fuck you guys," I said. "Everybody outside. Bring your whole fraternity outside and let's see what happens."

We left and walked to our car, glancing over our

shoulders through the flickering light from the street lamps to see if they were following us. I figured they were just frat douches and wouldn't have the guts to fight, even though they had us outnumbered.

But when we got about fifty yards down the street to Trevor's car, three guys came running out of the bar. Then more and more spilled out of the door, coming to fight.

I went to meet them, firing kicks. Trevor grabbed a tire iron from the back of his jeep and ran after me. I grabbed the tire iron from him—it was shaped like a PR-24, a combat baton I'd trained with in the Marines. A circle of fraternity brothers and onlookers formed around us. A couple of the frat boys started running their mouths, and it was clear this was going down. I fixed my eyes on the guy who seemed like the leader. His body language told me he was poised, like a snake, just looking for an opening to strike. With intensity, I whacked him on the leg with the tire iron—and then everyone started fighting at once.

Three guys jumped Trevor while three others attacked Billy. I waded in using the tire iron and cleared the guys off Trevor and then off Billy. Someone tackled me—I felt a sharp pain in my back, and then I was on the ground, loose gravel scraping my hands and face. My mind slowed things down, fighting for awareness. *Okay, there's Billy. Watch your six, Trevor!* It was an all-out melee now, a blur of punches flying and kicks exploding. We were blocking the street so traffic couldn't pass; the cold air filled with shouted curses and honking horns.

I got to my feet, turned around, and tossed one of the frat boys over the hood of an idling car. More confusion, more shouting, more fog as we fought all comers.

Then six police cruisers raced in, sirens blaring, and screeched to a halt.

The crowd scattered fast. We dashed to Trevor's car and drove away, shaking with adrenaline. Looking around, we surveyed the damage: we were bloody and bruised, our clothes torn. Someone had hit Trevor over the back with a club or nightstick, and he had a nasty welt. But we were all okay, and we'd left a dozen frat guys moaning on the pavement.

"We just kicked their asses!" we shouted over and over. It became our battle cry.

That car of Trevor's soon became a frequent subject of discussion. It was a Chevy Camaro Z28 that had once been a sharp ride, but he'd bent the front axle somehow and the computer system was broken to the point where the gas gauge and speedometer were always at zero. By age and mileage, he could have gotten a few thousand for the car. But in its current state, it was worthless.

One of us, I can't remember who, offered a plan. "If we made it look like it was stolen, and then it just 'disappeared,' the insurance company would pay up." It seemed so easy. And though I suppose we all knew that doing something like this would be a case of spectacularly bad judgment, we were tightknit and always had each other's backs.

After talking more over some beers, we decided we'd push the car into Lake Erie from an abandoned loading dock. A day later, late at night, we were ready to execute. As we piled out of Trevor's car, carefully leaving it in neutral, we closed the doors and started pushing it toward the water. We jumped when we heard a groan—the wood of the pier heaving under our weight. I don't know about the others, but my heart was beating so hard I could feel it in my ears. Finally, we got the car over the edge and into the water—big gurgles as the car began to sink. We didn't wait around to see it disappear.

We scattered—our plan was to rendezvous later. I ran in the shadows, crossing intersections and train tracks, until I reached a gas station. It was swarmed with cop cars. I didn't know who they were looking for—a shooter, a robber, a drunk driver—but I desperately hoped it wasn't me. I kept on running. I started seeing cop cars *everywhere.* By midnight, I realized I needed a ride. I called my dad. "Look, no questions asked," I said, "but I need you to come pick me up."

As soon as I got in the car, I told my dad what we'd done.

"That's fraud," he said. "A felony. Anybody see you?"

"I don't think so."

"You're going to need to stay low."

I couldn't sleep that night. What if someone had gotten hurt? What if we get caught?

My dad had told me he would watch the papers to make sure there had been no fallout. I called him a few days later. "Anything?" I asked.

"No," he said, "looks like you're good."

I let out a breath I hadn't realized I'd been holding. "Thank God," I said. "I can't believe we did that. Our lives could have changed forever."

"Looks like you got away with it," my dad said.

Our scheme had worked perfectly. No one had been hurt, and Trevor got a check from his insurance company.

But soon after that I started having a recurring nightmare: Billy, Trevor, and I were having a party and accidentally killed someone. All we could do was bury the body—*It was an accident*, we'd say to each other helplessly. Then the dream would fast-forward weeks, months, years, even decades. There I was, living a good life, successful and happy, and then this secret of my past would resurface and ruin me. The dread would settle over me like a thick mist, and I would wake up in a cold sweat. *I'm a murderer*, I would think, my heart pounding in my chest. Slowly, I'd fight my way back into reality from the nightmare's haze. I was not a murderer. No one had died.

. . .

When I got my grades for my first semester, I stared at the report—a 2.8 GPA—and tossed it on the coffee table.

"How bad it is?" Billy asked.

I nodded at the paper and Billy picked it up. Trevor rushed to look over his shoulder.

"Two point eight? Way to go, Johnny!" Trevor roared as Billy reached to give me a high five. "That's awesome!"

I loved these guys, but unlike them, I wasn't going to be happy with that GPA. Two-eight? Damn, I'd had BACs higher than that. I knew I could do better. I knew I could do more with my life.

That summer after my first semester, Billy, Trevor,

and I decided to become volunteer firefighters. We joked that this would make us chick magnets, but the truth was that I wanted to be a hero again.

Plus, I wasn't looking to attract women—I was dating Francesca, a black-haired Italian classmate who'd won me over with her sense of humor. Seeing me come out of the restroom once, she'd asked me wryly, "How's that burning sensation going for you?"

I kind of like this girl, I thought.

I was still wounded from what had happened with Tina, but Francesca was just getting out of a serious relationship herself, so we had an unspoken understanding—we would hang out all the time, enjoying each other's company, but it wasn't heavy.

What Fran *was* serious about was studying. She wanted to be a nurse. She and I started studying together, combing through our notes and reading passages aloud to each other. We made flash cards and quizzed each other. I was finally applying myself, and my grades showed it.

Plus, that fall I started taking courses I actually *enjoyed.* I was enrolled in a literature interpretation course. On the first day of class, the professor asked us what "apple" meant to us. I had no idea what he was talking about. An apple was an apple, a piece of fruit. But slowly, other students began chiming in. For some, an apple symbolized health. Others thought of a metropolis, the Big Apple. Still others saw original sin, like the apple Eve ate, or American values, as in apple pie. This was interesting to me, understanding how other people thought, the words they used. Taking that class, I started thinking about art—and life—in new ways. I saw that the key was connection, story. What did things *mean* to people?

I also started taking an emergency medical technician course, which was required and paid for by the fire department as part of my volunteering agreement.

Right away I loved it. Everything I was learning was something I might have to use at any time during my ambulance shifts—I could be called tomorrow to put direct pressure on a wound or splint somebody's leg. Our EMT professor showed us a video about why anyone would choose this stressful line of work. In the video, a high school football player went down on the field after a collision. His teammates started panicking when he didn't get up, and then his coach began CPR. The ambulance arrived and shocked him back to life, carting him off the field to waves of applause.

"We affect lives," my teacher concluded, shutting off the tape. "We drastically change people's lives." I fought back tears. *I want to do that*, I thought. *I want to change people's lives, to be the guy who comes in and saves the day.*

That semester, my GPA was a 3.8.

I was still drinking heavily, mostly because of my night gig as a bouncer. I'd been drinking at a '70s-themed bar and started talking to the owner—it turned out he was a kickboxing promoter and owned a gym. He invited me to train there, and eventually I started participating in paid fighting matches. Kickboxing for the bar owner was a bit of a transition—I was used to full-contact tae kwon do, and it took me a while to learn to keep my hands up. But I got better and better, even earning some money. Plus, the more I fought in the ring, the less I fought in bars and on the street.

Once this guy knew I could fight, he asked me to work the door at his club. It was an easy job, and I got along well with the bouncers. One bouncer, a guy named Big Al who weighed upwards of four hundred pounds, liked to get me drunk. I'd ask for a Jack Daniels and Coke and he'd come back with a glass of straight Jack.

I was drinking too much, but it didn't feel that way. I was just drinking as much as everyone around me—including my family. That Christmas, I went through the usual wringer: I started out at my mom's house, where everybody drank. When I announced I was headed to my dad's, the hysterics started. Explosions, tears, *How could you do this to me? After everything I've done for you?* Then, with my dad and Agnes, the steady, sterile, surface-only conversations.

Christmas was always hard, but this year I felt stronger, more equipped to deal with the waves crashing around me. I was training regularly, I was acing school, and I had a new plan: I was going to be a PA: a physician assistant. I'd heard about this career path from my upstairs neighbor, who was a paramedic. I had also talked about it with Francesca, who was now also considering becoming a PA instead of a nurse. A PA has considerably more skills and responsibilities than an EMT: could diagnose problems, prescribe medicine, refer to specialists. A PA does essentially the same work as a physician. They also got a much bigger paycheck to go along with the greater responsibility.

And if I missed the excitement of being an EMT, I could be an emergency room PA.

I was going to change people's lives.

But that spring semester, the course I was most excited about was public speaking, a class on the third floor of the college building. During our first class, our teacher, Professor Nash—a middle-aged guy with a huge shock of salt-and-pepper hair that was always standing at some funny angle—gave us an assignment: a simple introductory speech, three to five minutes long. We would deliver our speeches the next time class met. Professor Nash discussed with us the basics of a good speech, one that would engage the class. "I value feedback when it comes to improving, so you can expect to hear from each other," he said. "But don't attack my cubs."

We looked at him, confused.

"That's you," he said. "You're all my cubs, and you need to feel safe if you're going to learn."

I spent hours preparing my speech. During the next class, Professor Nash had an audio recorder set up. He appointed an "Um Master," someone to keep track of how many times speakers slipped and said "um" or "er."

"Well," he said, rubbing his palms together. "Who wants to go first?"

My hand shot up. He beckoned me to the front of the room, and I stood up straight in front of my classmates. "Professor Nash, my fellow classmates," I began, "my name's John Bielinski. Carpe diem, seize the day. That's my motto, and this is my story."

I told them about how much I'd always loved martial arts. I told them how I'd been a peace-love-hug-a-tree kind of guy when I was younger. I told them about Billy getting shot; they gasped. I told them about becoming a fighter and joining the Marines. I told them about leaving my family to go away to war. I told them about that first firefight.

"I thought I was going to die," I said, placing a hand on my heart. "I mean I really, truly thought I was going to die." I shook my head, allowed a beat of silence. "I thought I was going to *die.*"

I finished by describing my evolution: I was going to become a healer. I was going to help people. "I want to get into the medical field," I said, "probably to become a PA." I looked out into my classmates' faces and smiled broadly. "Thank you," I said.

They erupted into applause. When I took my seat, the girl behind me squeezed my shoulder. "I thought I was gonna cry," she said.

Professor Nash stood up, still clapping, and stopped the video recorder. "Wonderful," he said. "Such effective use of repetition." I hadn't even realized that repetition was a strategy—it just felt right, a way to connect with the audience.

While I might have inadvertently discovered a talent for connecting with groups, my one-on-one relationships weren't going so well.

Not long after my speech triumph, Francesca and I celebrated her birthday—but she left early. I had a bad feeling. The next day, on a hunch, I asked, "Did you go back to your old boyfriend?"

She looked at me guiltily.

"Okay," I said. "Okay."

"It was just a one-time thing," she said. "I don't want this to wreck what we have."

But this was a deal-breaker for me. "We are done," I said coldly, and walked away.

Big Al got me especially drunk at work that night, and I came to class the next day nursing a killer hangover even while I was still a little drunk. I got to public speaking class early, silently cursing the harsh fluorescent lighting and doing my best not to throw up.

Francesca showed up a few minutes later, taking a seat in the row in front of me. She reeked of Obsession—a perfume I'd always hated and she knew it.

"*Hey*," she said to me as I lifted my head up.

She turned around.

"You smell *disgusting*," I said.

Then, nauseated by the smell, unable to sit there a second longer, I went to the gym and passed out on the hardwood floor. I woke up with a splitting headache, remembering what I'd said.

On some level, I knew I was at a crossroads. I was making good grades. I was training hard. I wanted a career in medicine. The puzzle pieces of my life were starting to fit together. But I was still drinking, still occasionally getting into fights.

I quit my job at the bar and doubled down on my studies, determined not to slip now that I'd lost my study partner. I'd let a girlfriend derail my life before— that wasn't going to happen again.

In public speaking class, we were assigned partners— mine was a shy yet serious girl with long blond hair named Sheri—and told to conduct a debate in front of the class.

"What do you think we should do?" Sheri asked me during our planning time.

"I think we should debate whether girls or guys are responsible for all the trouble in relationships," I said, stealing a glance at Francesca, whose back felt turned specifically to me. "I think it would get the class really *engaged*."

Before our debate, Sheri and I had beers in the school parking lot. "To men versus women," I said, clinking our bottles.

In class, I channeled all my anger and frustration into the debate, controlling it, adding just the right amount of humor, playing the crowd.

"All men want to do is have sex and then move on," Sheri said.

"Well, maybe you should be more choosy about who you sleep with," I countered.

The women in the class gasped collectively. They glared. They *hated* me. By the end of the debate, though, I'd accomplished exactly what I'd set out to do. I got people to *feel* something. I didn't want to just deliver information, I wanted to create an emotional experience. Mission accomplished.

When the period was over, a friend of mine from class approached me. He smiled and said, "You're pretty good at getting people's attention."

"Hey, thanks," I said.

He fished something out of his pocket: a cassette tape. "I think you'd like this," he said, handing it to me. "Don't worry about returning it."

I thanked him again and looked down at the tape.

It was an audiobook: Anthony Robbins, *Awaken the Giant Within: Take Immediate Control of Your Mental, Emotional, Physical, and Financial Destiny.* I slipped it into my pocket. A week or so later, when I was packing for spring break—a friend and I were headed to Panama City, Florida, for the week—I put the tape in the glove box along with the others we'd be listening to on the car ride: Journey, Supertramp. I figured we could use any entertainment we could get for the long ride.

On the drive, I took a turn at the wheel at night, the green mile-marker signs pulling us southward. Somewhere south of Nashville, my friend fell asleep. I was getting sick of Journey. After fishing around through the pile of tapes in the dark, I popped the Robbins cassette into the tape deck. His voice came through the speakers, keeping me company as I sped along the desolate highway.

Immediately I was riveted. What Anthony Robbins was describing was just what I wanted— control, stability, power. I soaked up everything I heard, weaving it together with my own situation and goals. I considered my private dream of becoming not just a PA, but a doctor. What stood in my way? *Sure, it's great to want to be a doctor. But you're not smart enough, Johnny boy. Not by half. So what if you aced English lit? How do you think you would do in anatomy with all that Latin?*

At age twenty-three, I imagined how life would unfold if I stayed chained to my self-limiting beliefs. *Thirty years old, still just scraping by, one medical emergency or car malfunction away from financial ruin.*

Underachieving at dead-end jobs, wondering whether this was all there was to life.

In this same near-hypnotized state, I imagined what could happen if I embraced a life free of negative self-talk, a life where I felt like I was good enough. *Working hard, but loving every second. John Bielinski, MD. A healer, using knowledge and intuition to help people restore their health.*

No question, I liked the look of life without limits. And while I knew that school had never been easy for me, I also knew that, like my father, I could outwork anyone. *No one's going to work harder than me—no one.*

I had to ground my feelings in tangible action. I had to put words to my dream to keep it alive. As soon as I got back from spring break, I went to the University at Buffalo School of Medicine and Biomedical Sciences bookstore and bought a bumper sticker. I carefully cut out the letters and rearranged them. On my rear windshield, I spelled it out for all to see: "Med School or Bust."

Chapter 6

Dream Change

After that night when the Robbins tape awakened my own personal giant within, I was all about school—I felt impatient, like I'd been rehearsing for a performance and I couldn't wait to get up on stage in front of an actual audience. As well as I was doing at community college, I wanted to break out and show what I could do at a competitive four-year school. After spring break, I finished the semester strong, and then took anatomy and physiology over the summer.

Then, after one more semester at Erie Community College, I went straight into the University at Buffalo for the spring 1994 semester, bound and determined to become a killer candidate for med school.

I knew I was going to have to minimize distractions, so I got my own place near campus—it was just a single bare room with dirty tile floors, a closet, and a community bathroom. I didn't have a desk, so I nailed a wide piece of plywood into a couple of old nightstands and set it near my one small window.

With a black permanent marker, I scrawled motivational quotes across the bare wood surface:

We can do, have, and be exactly what we wish.
—Anthony Robbins

Perpetual optimism is a force multiplier.
—Colin Powell

We are what we repeatedly do. Excellence, then, is not an act, but a habit.
—Aristotle

I wanted these thoughts, these affirmations, to be on my mind constantly, driving me forward.

I was going to need them.

The classroom competition at the university was no joke. Classes were much larger than they had been at Erie, and I was surprised at all the international students; the university was elite enough to draw top students from around the world. I had moved from a small pond into an ocean—but now I knew how to swim. My time at community college had allowed me to learn from small classes, gain tenacity, and build confidence. Erie had given me momentum, kinetic energy—it had turned the key in the ignition.

I struggled in the tougher math and science classes, but I was determined to work harder than everybody.

Every night I'd make a full pot of the strongest coffee possible, and then I'd stay in my room like a hermit, studying till two or three in the morning. When I was exhausted but couldn't sleep, still jittery from the coffee, I'd come down with a few shots of Jack. I was drinking alone, but I didn't feel lonely—I felt in control, like I'd figured out the strategy.

I stopped partying as much: I had a laser focus on my schoolwork, yes, but also, at twenty-four, college bars started feeling too young for me. Plus, Billy had moved an hour away for a new job, and he may as well have moved to Mars—I barely ever saw him.

But on weekends and in between exams, I found ways to blow off steam.

One night I went with a friend to a place with a dance bar downstairs and a piano bar upstairs. I headed downstairs and was a couple of drinks in when I saw her: a petite, athletic-looking woman with curly brown hair. She was bubbly, vivacious, bouncing from one foot to the other.

I made my way over to her. "Buy you a drink?"

She laughed. "Don't you want to know my name first?"

"Before, after ... My name's John, and we're going to have fun tonight."

"My name's Tricia," she said. "Prove it."

I got us a couple of Jack and Cokes, grabbed Tricia by the hand, and led her upstairs to the piano bar. Two pianists were just beginning to play "Crocodile Rock." I handed Tricia my drink and hopped up on the little stage with the musicians.

"I remember when rock was young," I belted. "Me

and—Tricia—had so much fun." Tricia laughed.

I don't remember too much about the rest of the night, but I know we had fun—just as I'd promised. And make no mistake, I killed it at karaoke.

I started spending some time with Tricia after that, but it wasn't serious. She worked a nine-to-five job, and she often tried to get me to stay out late or blow off studying. But I drew a hard line: Grades were everything. Becoming a doctor was everything. She did get me to play on her co-ed volleyball and softball teams, and we'd go out to eat sometimes.

Tricia also liked to come watch my kickboxing training and fights. I remember one match vividly: I was in an important fight, and scores of my friends had come to watch. Tricia was there, whooping and cheering.

This guy I was fighting was tough. A strong boxer. But I pressed him with a pounding pace and tempo, firing booming punches and kicks and taking plenty in return, though my adrenaline was so high I barely felt them. Deep in the first round, we both began firing harder and harder, an aggressive engagement that ended with a sickening crack: I'd broken his arm.

I won the match by technical knockout. Although I usually loved the fanfare of being in combat, I felt shaky after that one. I hadn't broken the guy's arm on purpose, and I didn't feel great about that win.

But when I went over to Tricia after the match, she looked at me with wide-eyed wonder. She seemed impressed, admiring—more like a fan than a girlfriend, as though I were larger than life to her. Something about that look worried me, like she wanted something from me I couldn't give her.

And yes: quickly, things with Tricia got harder and more complicated. She created drama just to get a reaction out of me. If I didn't call her, she'd leave me incessant voicemail messages. Once, when we were out to dinner, she looked at me over her grilled chicken breast and said, "John, I'm pregnant." I froze, my fork halfway to my mouth. *This can't be happening*, I thought. *I know she's on the pill, I've seen the little compact she keeps in her purse.* My thoughts raced, and my heart hammered in my chest.

Tricia burst into laughter and lifted a bite to her mouth. "Gotcha," she crowed. "Your face! Would it really be so bad if I were pregnant?"

"Yeah, you're a real comedian," I said.

In May, toward the end of my first semester, I tried to end things with Tricia. We weren't right together, I could see that, and school was kicking my ass. I'd dropped physics when my grades dipped, figuring I would take it in the summer, but I knew I needed to work even harder.

So one night, when she started trying to create drama, I'd had it—and told her so. I was out. I turned off my answering machine. I didn't answer or return Tricia's calls.

A week later, when I returned to my room after class, I found a bunch of red, yellow, and orange balloons tied to my door and some sunflowers in a vase on the floor. When I brought them inside, their bright colors and sunniness really perked up my little room, and it reminded me of what I liked about Tricia. I decided to give her another chance. After all, she was a lot of fun, and she made me feel good about myself. Plus, I reasoned, I was working as hard as I could, and I needed to balance it out with *some* fun.

I completed my first semester at Buffalo with a 3.2 GPA. This was a competitive number—my dream was still alive. Knowing professors were more lax with grading during the summer, I carefully arranged to take the toughest required classes then.

Soon after my summer courses started, I found myself in a bar one late Friday afternoon. I'd had a hard week, and I self-medicated with beer and chicken wings. When I finally stepped up to leave, I felt a telltale sway: too drunk to drive. Well, what the hell—I decided to drive anyway. The bar was in a shitty section of Buffalo, and I wasn't wild about the idea of leaving the car there overnight. Besides, Tricia was expecting me.

But about halfway to Tricia's, I saw flashing lights in my rearview mirror. *Shit.* I carefully pulled to the side of the road, fished out my license and insurance, and waited.

"Do you realize you were going forty-seven miles per hour in a thirty-five zone?" the officer asked me.

"No, I'm sorry," I said. "I was thinking about my classes and my girlfriend." I smiled.

He squinted into approaching headlights. "This is a tricky stretch of highway," he said gruffly. "Go ahead and follow me back to my squad car."

I focused: *Walk straight, act casual.* After I closed the cruiser door, I let out a sigh.

The officer looked at me sharply. "You been drinking, sir?"

My gut twisted, but I knew lying wouldn't help. "Yes," I said. "Yes, I have."

He kept his eyes on me; I knew he was thinking about whether it would be worth his while to take me in on a DWI. Then he opened his ticket book, scribbled for a moment, and handed me my license, insurance card, and a ticket—for failure to wear a seat belt. "Keep your speed down and stay safe," he said. He jerked his head, telling me to go.

I gave him what I hoped was a grateful, contrite smile before walking quickly back to my car, starting it, and driving away. *I just got away with it*, I thought. *Again. Jesus. One of these days I'm going to get arrested—or end up in the hospital. Or God, I could kill someone.* My heart beat heavily, as if I hadn't gotten away with anything.

I got to Tricia's house, still feeling the beer and the stress of being pulled over. I cut the engine, opened the door, and just sat for a moment with my head in my hands, breathing in the cool summer evening. After a few more deep breaths, I walked to Tricia's door.

She opened it, grinning. "John," she said, leaning up to give me a kiss. "Come sit down with me." She led me to her flowered couch and sat next to me, eyes bright. "I have some news," she said. "I'm pregnant."

For a moment, my vision swam, then snapped back to clarity. "Very funny," I said. "I've gotta be honest, Tricia, I'm really not in the mood for jokes."

Her smile held, though it tightened a bit. "I'm not joking."

"Nope," I said. "Not possible. I've had a long week and I've got no time for games. We're going to buy a test together, right now. Get your bag."

"Are you serious?"

"I'm serious."

At the drugstore, she selected a box. "Let's get two," I said harshly, grabbing another. In the checkout line, I fumbled to get my credit card out of my wallet. I was still drunk.

Back at Tricia's apartment, I watched her pee on one stick, then another. She set both tests on the sink and we stared at each other. She was still smiling; I felt a mixture of anger and panic. *She thinks she's funny,* I thought. When the time was up, we looked down at the tests. She beamed, but I closed my eyes and squeezed the bridge of my nose with my right hand.

Tricia was pregnant.

Recently, she had played volleyball in the rain and come down with bronchitis. "The antibiotic my doctor gave me must have made my birth control fail," Tricia said.

I lay down on the bed. *That's it. My dream of becoming a doctor is done.* I wallowed in a mixture of anger and self-pity until the beer caught up with me and I was fast asleep.

I woke up the next morning as if from a bad dream, jittery and unsettled. I had a dull headache, and the sunlight streaming through the blinds seemed harsh. As I wiped the sleep from my eyes and the haze wore off, reality set in: I'd dodged a DWI. Tricia was pregnant. *Tricia's pregnant. Why couldn't I have gotten the DWI instead?*

In bed next to me, Tricia's chest rose and fell with

each soft breath. I stared at the ceiling. *I can't believe I'm here. I can't believe she's pregnant. How could this happen?*

The next few days were tense between us. We had the same conversation over and over again. "I'm pregnant, so you marry me," she'd say. "That's what happens."

"I'm not marrying you," I'd say. "I'll be the baby's dad, but I'm not changing my plans."

Eventually, Tricia realized she had to change her strategy. "You need to talk with my parents," she said.

Three days later, I sat with Tricia and her parents, Patty and Glenn, in their modest, neat living room outside Niagara Falls, New York. My eyes wandered around the room, taking in the porcelain figures arranged on a bookshelf and the copies of *Time* stacked on the coffee table.

I cleared my throat. "As I told Tricia, I fully intend to take care of the baby and to support your daughter," I said. "But I'm not getting married."

Patty looked down at her hands and shook her head. "I'm so happy Tricia's pregnant, but I'm embarrassed to tell my friends she won't be married," she said.

You're embarrassed? *Fuck that. I have plans. I told Tricia from the beginning that school comes first.*

Glenn, a barrel-chested Italian with a hard set to his mouth, caught my eye and held my gaze. "The thing is," he began before pausing. "If you're not going to get married, I'm going to tell Tricia to have an abortion."

My stomach dropped. I looked at Tricia, whose face told me that her father spoke for her.

There was still a big part of me that was in pain because I wasn't over Tina—and even more than that, because I wasn't able to be a father to Corey. I *wanted* to be a dad. Sometimes I saw dads with their kids—riding bikes, eating ice cream cones—and tears came to my eyes, picturing Corey doing these things without me. The thought of not being there for another child was unacceptable. Maybe I had a choice, but it didn't feel that way. I felt backed into a corner.

The next day, I went to my dad for an eye exam and told him I was going to marry Tricia.

"You're making a big mistake, Johnny," he said. "Big mistake."

This may have been his idea of help, but it didn't help me. Who was my father, anyway, to judge me for trying to do the right thing?

A few weeks later, in July, Tricia and I got married in her parents' backyard under a pop-up tent by a minister who lived down the street. He didn't know she was pregnant; she wasn't showing yet. Rain poured down through the whole ceremony and reception. Tricia smiled and laughed, and I tried to fight off a sense of dread. *Maybe we'll make it work*, I thought desperately. *Maybe a baby will change everything.*

At the reception following the ceremony, some family friends, the Johnsons, stopped by to talk. The Johnsons had known me since I was a baby; in fact, I'd once had Mrs. Johnson as a substitute teacher in third grade, where she'd caught me cheating on an assignment. Meanwhile, the Johnson kids had been strong, upstanding students.

"So what are your plans?" Mr. Johnson said. "I heard you're at Buffalo."

"I'm studying to get into medicine," I told him. "I'm going to apply to med school."

Their faces froze somewhere between a polite, astonished smile and a grimace of amused pity. It was a look that said: *Oh, that's so cute. But what are you* really *going to do when you grow up?*

It wasn't the first time someone had doubted me. It just gave me more fuel.

Following the wedding, Tricia and I moved into an apartment over a consignment shop. It was large enough for us to have a nursery and for me to have a real study. And I studied incessantly, pulling lots of all-nighters and hiring tutors. Going into that fall semester, my GPA had been a 3.4, and I was determined to keep it there.

I was still going full throttle, determined that this marriage and this baby wouldn't derail me. Looking back, though, it almost seems like I sabotaged myself: I had signed up for a whopping twenty-one credit hours—including the dreaded physics class that still hung over my head—and was working as a volunteer fireman on an ambulance, all while Tricia and I got ready for the baby to arrive.

Not only was I committed to going to med school, now I was also committed to being the hunter-gatherer-protector for my family. We'd found out the baby was a boy—I was going to have a son. I wanted to be there in the room when he was born; I wanted to feel the seismic shift of becoming a father.

Working on the ambulance, I wanted to learn as much as I could. One advantage to growing up feeling stupid was that I wasn't afraid to *look* stupid.

I constantly questioned the medics, asking why they did this or that. On one call, the medic looked up from the patient and said, "Holy cow, Bielinski. You're a pain in the ass to work with." But my attitude and knowledge got me known as "the good one," the one the paid professional medics always wanted to work with. Eventually, because of my reputation, I was given a paying job. This meant I was working the ambulance much more, twenty hours a week. I was in and out of hospitals, seeing car accidents, seeing babies born, doing CPR.

I was gaining valuable experience, but I was also overextending myself. My grades started slipping, and I had to withdraw from physics yet again, putting it off until the spring. When that spring semester came, I kept on trying to juggle everything, knowing that in a matter of weeks, our baby boy would arrive and throw things into even greater chaos.

On February 16, 1995, Tricia went into labor. That afternoon I was scheduled for a make-or-break physics midterm. As I sat with Tricia in the hospital, her labor stretching hour upon hour, I felt torn. I knew I could probably go to class, take the exam, and still be back in time for the birth. But I also knew I'd never forgive myself if I was wrong and missed the delivery.

I stayed.

Eventually, the obstetrician decided the labor had gone on long enough and delivered our son by caesarean section. After he was cleaned, weighed, and swaddled, the nurse handed him to me. Here was John David Bielinski in my arms. I was a father. He felt so light in my hands as I took him in: his dark eyes opening occasionally, eyelids fluttering; his light, downy hair already curling up underneath the cloth cap the nurses had placed on his head; his heart beating like a frightened rabbit's. I waited for the seismic shift to happen, expecting to be flooded instantly with love and purpose. Instead, I felt like I was living someone else's life, a spectator in my own life's drama.

My physics professor didn't want to give me a makeup exam, which enraged me. I fought for it hard, eventually going to the chairman of the department—and won.

Then I bombed the exam, and by now it was too late to drop the class. I'd get a failing grade for the semester.

As the weeks slipped by, a cloud of work, baby care, and Tricia's near-constant drama put me in a fog at school. Eventually, I saw there was a very real possibility I would fail not just physics but multiple classes.

I faced facts. I had to have a bachelor's degree to apply to med school, but after this catastrophic semester, my GPA would never recover enough to get me in. I had to change my tactics, and I had to move fast, before this semester's bad grades pulled my GPA to the floor. I could still become a physician assistant, because PA schools had looser requirements. I could still do the things I loved, still provide for my family. I could salvage my dream, even though it would look a little different than it once had.

But I had to apply now, before the semester grades were posted.

As I filled out applications for five PA schools, I felt

more like a file than a person. Everyone had a resume, a transcript, a number. How was I supposed to stand out from the other applicants?

I decided that one way to stand out was through my essay. I came up with a way to highlight my Marine Corps service, and everything flowed from there. The essay began:

"Wake up, Bielinski." That's what my teachers told me throughout high school. But my wake-up call came from the bugles of the US Marine Corps.

It was a strong essay. I also remembered the speech I'd given in the public speaking class at community college—about crossing into Kuwait, *knowing* I was going to die, and living instead, deciding to dedicate my life to health care. I had the speech on tape, so I made copies and slipped them in with my applications.

In the anxious weeks that followed, I rifled through the mail each day, hoping to hear back. Grades would be posted soon, so my window of opportunity was closing quickly.

Eventually, I received interview offers from four PA schools. I accepted three. Of those, I received two acceptance letters. When I got the first one, tears sprang to my eyes. Yet again, I'd dodged a bullet. But I was still holding out for news from the school I really wanted to go to: King's College in Wilkes-Barre, Pennsylvania, one of the most prestigious PA programs in the nation.

As I went through the mail in our tiny kitchen one spring evening, my breath caught: a crest in the upper-left corner of the envelope and the words "King's College." My heart beating like I was in a fight, I fumbled with the envelope, trying to open it without tearing the letter inside.

Oh no. I was on the wait list.

I was disappointed, but I decided to hold out hope. Besides, I still had options at two other schools. Just two days later, though, I received another letter from King's College.

"Dear Mr. Bielinski,

We are delighted to inform you that you've been accepted as a member of the King's College Department of Physician Assistant Studies for the Fall 1995 class ..."

I set the letter on the coffee table and closed my eyes, grinning broadly. I pounded the table with my fist. *Yes!* But then I froze in a moment of panic. Was I *definitely* in, or was my acceptance conditional pending this semester's grades?

I had to be sure—rock-solid sure. So the next day I drove the two hundred and fifty miles to Wilkes-Barre and visited the admissions office. I handed my now crumpled acceptance letter to a smiling assistant dean. "Is this real?"

She glanced at the letter and her smile grew wider. "It sure is. I processed this myself when we got an opening."

I pulled out my checkbook.

She let out a short laugh. "You don't pay me," she

said. "You need to go to the registrar's office—back out the door, down the hallway, second door on the left." She paused. "Congratulations, and welcome to King's College."

I went directly to the registrar's office and cut a check for registration. I didn't want anything to get in the way of this happening. I knew I'd gotten lucky and had snuck my way into a great school.

As I drove back to Buffalo, past sprawling pastures filled with cows, I thought about the journey I was on. It was true I wouldn't realize my dream of becoming a doctor, but I was still going to help people, heal people, save people. I was going to make a difference.

I imagined getting home, walking into Johnny's nursery, and lifting him gently from his crib. I imagined tucking him into the crook of my arm and looking down at his tiny face, his gummy smile. I hadn't been ready to be a father, but now, with the weight of uncertainty off me, I looked at my life, and Johnny, with new eyes. *That little boy is mine. I'm a dad—who just got into the best damn PA school in America!* He deserved a good life and all the chances in the world, and it was my job to give him that life and those chances.

I would do whatever it took.

Chapter 7

Drinking from a Fire Hose

I'm sure you know that line: "It was the best of times, it was the worst of times." Well, that's what my life was like for the next few years.

I was as excited about getting into the King's College PA program as I'd been about anything in my life. I'd been told I needed to buy a medical terminology book and master it because there would be a test on terms the first day of class. So I put all the words on flash cards and studied them constantly all summer long, any time I had a free moment—even while I worked my ambulance shifts.

And I loved being a dad to Johnny. There's just something about a baby's giggle—Johnny's giggle. Every day I'd swoop him into my arms and cuddle him, feeling the softness of his skin, marveling that this human being was a part of me. Stroking his downy hair and looking into his wide dark eyes, it was impossible not to feel a sense of optimism and hope for the future.

But I was still married to Tricia. At the time, maybe I'd have said I was still trying to find equilibrium in my marriage—but really I was just going through the motions. I hadn't wanted to get married to Tricia in the first place, and actually being married to her hadn't done anything to change my mind. She was a good woman who deserved more: after working, studying, and caring for Johnny, I didn't have much of anything to give to Tricia. But even without my obligations, I wouldn't have been able to give her what she needed from me. I just didn't spark with her, and increasingly we were civil and polite to each other but without a greater sense of any kind of "us." Although I tried to set it aside, living with her was an increasing strain.

Tricia was family-oriented, and in that summer before we moved to Wilkes-Barre, she wanted to spend lots of time at her parents' house. I would dutifully go with her, but I didn't like it. Glenn and Patty were good people; I just didn't have much in common with them.

An image sticks out in my mind from their house: They had some scuffed-up linoleum square flooring, and one piece went spinning across the room every time you walked on it. I would send it flying, and they would graciously tell me not to worry—just set it back in place. It bothered me so much, this broken thing they could have fixed with a buck's worth of adhesive. But it didn't bother them at all. They were content to live life as it was, without change, without improvement. Not me. So I would just sit there with my flash cards, trying to conceal my annoyance at having to be there.

Finally, the time came for us to move. Tricia and I found a duplex a mile from school; I liked the idea of being able to walk and not having to worry about driving and parking. Plus, I wanted Tricia to have the car so she could get Johnny around, especially in case of emergency.

Wilkes-Barre was a blue-collar town, and we lived on a blue-collar street occupied mostly by workers, with a sprinkling of students. It was a low-rent area, but I always felt safe there. It was a shotgun apartment, narrow and deep, about six feet wide and thirty feet long. We had two bedrooms—one of which we converted into a nursery—a bathroom, a kitchen, and a small room in the front with a couch and television. A high fence in the backyard gave us privacy if we wanted to grill some burgers. It wasn't fancy, but it was affordable and provided for our basic needs. Once our household was squared away, I bought my books and nervously waited for the first day of class.

I'll never forget walking into a small lecture hall my first day with the forty other students who made up my class. The air was filled with nervous excitement. Voices hummed as clusters of students introduced themselves and took their seats.

Precisely at eight a.m., Dr. Eleanor Babonis, the program director, walked to the lectern. She had short red hair, a grandmotherly figure with broad shoulders. After introducing herself, she braced us for what we'd signed up for.

"This program is like drinking water from a fire hose,"

she said. "It's not easy, and we have high standards. In this program, an eighty is passing—not a seventy."

This sounded tough—but she went on to explain that at this school, we'd have support. If we worked hard, the school would make sure we succeeded. I liked the sound of this—I liked the idea of that kind of support.

Still, I wasn't complacent. Along with everyone else in that lecture hall, I understood that the school would help us if we were truly making an honest effort. I knew they'd have no problem throwing me out on my ass if I was just coasting.

I also figured I would have to work harder than anybody else to begin with. I felt like it was clear to all my classmates and professors that I wasn't supposed to be there. I was certain it was only a matter of time before King's College got hold of my transcript from my last semester at University of Buffalo and tossed me out of the program. It was a little like the fear I'd lived with for months after dumping Trevor's car in Lake Erie—I just knew I'd be found out. And once I was, all my dreams would be dashed.

One day in my epidemiology class, my professor described something called "imposter syndrome"—when a person lives in fear of being exposed as a fraud. I was startled. *That's me*, I thought. *That's what I have.* Those days of being pulled out of class for "special education"—they had never truly left me.

But here was the twist: this feeling of being inadequate, like I was some kind of faker, might have held me back—but instead I'd made it jet fuel for my studies. I was just so damn happy I'd gotten into the program in the first place that I worked my ass off.

I had to, because Dr. Babonis hadn't been kidding about the flood of material we were expected to master. School days stretched from eight in the morning to six in the evening. Clinical medicine, physical diagnoses, dermatology, ophthalmology, medical ethics, epidemiology, reading x-rays and EKGs: I knew there was no way I could possibly keep up with everything.

My solution was to bust my ass on clinical medicine topics, which I figured I would need to know inside and out to be an effective PA. Outside of that, I would do the minimum I had to, relying on Dr. Babonis's promise that the school would help anyone who wasn't passing.

Even choosing to focus on just the essentials, I was studying constantly. If my marriage had been difficult before, now it was impossible.

Sometimes Tricia was sweet, trying to convince me to watch a movie or go out with her and the baby. "I can't," I would say weakly. "I have to study."

"That's what you always say," she'd respond with sad eyes.

But many other times, instead of getting sad, she got angry. She did whatever she thought she needed to do to get my attention. If we had an argument that stretched out into the night, she refused to let me sleep, poking me in the shoulder. "*You* may have a test tomorrow," she said, "but I can do this all night."

During another argument, she started pushing and prodding me. I backed away from her, hoping her anger would subside. She kept advancing, walking into my space in a way I would never allow a guy to do. Her nostrils flared and her eyes narrowed as she taunted me: "Hit me. Go on, hit me. You know you want to."

I held my arms tightly at my sides, staring at her incredulously.

I see now that Tricia must have felt so isolated, staying home with Johnny all day, her family far away—but at the time, I wasn't thinking about that. I was struggling to keep my head above water. It seemed to me that this was what she'd signed on for. *She had to have known how things would be between us,* I told myself.

Very quickly, it started feeling like I was leading two separate lives: my life at school, where I was pouring myself out, and my life at home, where I had nothing left to give, even if I'd wanted to give it. Any intimacy Tricia and I had shared drained away, leaving only numbness and routine.

Tricia and I were both lonely at home, but at school I soon found some fellow students to form a study group with. Kathy was a hard worker, studying even harder than I did—she even worked while in PA school. This was frowned upon by the program, but Kathy was enough of a workhorse that she could handle it. Pam was more of a people person, and she warmed to my study style. Sometimes we were joined by Pam and Kathy's friend Michelle, who stayed on the group's periphery, doing her own thing.

I found something special, almost magical, about studying with others—it brought out the best in me. I would review incredibly complicated material and think, *How can I explain this to the rest of the group?*

By figuring out how I could most effectively *teach* the material, I would master it.

My teaching method was patient-oriented. So, say we were studying heart attacks. I'd say something like, "Okay, paramedics deliver a fifty-year-old man with an apparent heart attack. What is this man going to look like? What symptoms does he have?" We were constantly talking like that, focusing on how patients would present clinically. And by preparing well enough to teach my study mates, I got the material down cold.

When we weren't in class or at home, the four of us were probably studying together; we became known as "Johnny's Angels," a nod to the TV show "Charlie's Angels." Although it could have been awkward—a married man studying with three attractive single women—it wasn't, because we were all so focused and driven.

Even so, because Pam was so gullible, we did have a bit of fun at her expense from time to time.

One day after a class on congestive heart failure, we tested each other on our professor's lecture. As we ticked off symptoms, I softly kicked Michelle and Kathy under the table. "Oh yeah, I almost forgot," I began. "The patient's eyeballs turn blue."

"What?" Pam said. "I didn't get that."

"That's right," Kathy said.

"I can't believe we almost forgot that," Michelle added.

"I must have completely zoned out," Pam said, scanning her notebook. "I didn't even write that down."

I think it's only natural we had that kind of camaraderie. During that long first year, we spent more time with each other than with anyone else. I know that had to be hard for Tricia. She was with a baby all day without friends or family to support her. I loved being in class, and I loved coming home to Johnny. But I just didn't feel anything for Tricia, and I mostly tolerated her. I know saying that does me no credit. Tricia was a good person, but I just didn't love her and I didn't have it in me to pretend.

That's not to say I was incapable of romantic feelings.

As Johnny's Angels spent hour upon hour with each other, I began to feel a spark with Michelle. Of course she was pretty—slim and fierce with long, dark hair—but it was more than that. She had an independent streak, a sharp tongue, and a strong, opinionated nature.

During one study session, as we quizzed each other on paralysis, I tossed down my note cards. "You know," I said, "if I ever became paralyzed, I'd rather die."

Michelle put down her pen and sat back in her chair. She fixed me with her steady gaze and said, "Pretty shortsighted."

"How so?" I asked.

"Wouldn't you want to be at your son's graduation? See him get married?"

I stared at her. "I guess I never thought of it that way." I liked that—I liked how she could help me see the world differently.

Still, we were just study partners. The four of us usually met in small, glass-walled library cubicles, but once a week we'd meet at someone's house to study and have dinner together. When it was my turn to host, there wasn't any awkwardness between Tricia and the

Angels. Tricia joined us for the meal but stayed with Johnny while we studied.

But maybe I was just fooling myself. One day I joined Kathy and Pam in the library. As I unpacked my books and note cards, I idly asked whether Michelle was going to be joining us.

"I don't know," Pam said. Then, slyly, she added, "You know, you guys would make a great couple."

"Oh my God, I was thinking the same thing," Kathy said.

I was caught off guard. "I'm married, I've got a kid," I said. "What are you talking about?"

"It happens," Kathy said.

I hurried to change the subject. "I have a new mnemonic for us to remember aortic regurgitation," I said. But as we studied, I kept on thinking about Michelle.

In fact, I couldn't stop thinking about her.

Meanwhile, all the studying paid off: I was a high-B student. And at the end of the semester, I was ready for a break. My fellow classmates were, too. Someone had organized a Christmas party after finals, a gathering at a quiet bar for some drinks and dancing before people left for the month-long break, which Tricia, Johnny, and I would spend in Buffalo. Up until this point, I had consciously been pushing away my growing interest in Michelle, but now it really hit me that I wouldn't be seeing her for a month.

At the dark, noisy bar, Michelle and I talked in a general way; I felt awkward and constrained, but I just wanted to spend time with her. A couple of hours later, when the party started breaking up, Michelle stood up from her bar stool. "Well," she said uncertainly, "I guess I'll see you in a month!"

"Yeah, that'll be good," I replied, feeling a little panicked. "But—you want to hang out a while longer? Maybe go over to the American Legion hall and shoot pool?"

She smiled. "What are the stakes?"

"Oh, you want to bet?"

"Just something to make it more interesting," she said. "Let's say the loser has to reveal a personal truth."

As we walked to the hall, downtown Christmas lights glittering down on us through the falling snow, I was confident that I'd be learning something I didn't know about Michelle. After playing so much pool with my dad, I was a pretty good shot.

But it wasn't long after I'd racked the balls that I saw I'd been sharked: Michelle won.

At a small, beat-up table, on folding chairs, we sipped our beers. Michelle looked at me expectantly. "Well?"

I cleared my throat.

"I'm so attracted to you it's blowing my mind," I blurted.

Michelle's eyes widened. Wordlessly, she took my hands in hers.

We ended up at Michelle's house, and although we didn't have sex, we made out with a semester's worth of suppressed passion. After a few hours, as I prepared to leave, sadness and confusion washed over me. This was before cell phones and email, and the thought of going a month without any kind of communication with

Michelle filled me with loneliness. "Bye," I said, pulling her close one last time. "See you in a month."

The next morning, as Tricia and I packed up the car and drove home to Buffalo, my mind was in torment. *What have I gotten into? Where is this going? I want to be a good guy—but does that mean working to save a marriage I never wanted, even though it's just a shell?* I looked at Johnny through the rearview mirror. *But I've got a son I love more than anything or anyone. I can't risk that, can I?*

Since my parents' divorce, Christmases were usually full of sadness and hurt feelings, but this one was a fog; I was sleepwalking. I was in a surreal situation and didn't know what was happening. I talked to Tricia like I had since we got married—playing the role of a good husband. Our communication was superficial, and I was distracted by thoughts about Michelle. I was just numb.

When we finally drove back to Wilkes-Barre for the spring semester, I felt flooded with relief. I would soon be absorbed in studying the topics I loved—and I'd get to see Michelle again.

And once I saw her, my heart knew what it wanted. We still didn't know what the future held, but we were both excited to explore what could be, exchanging love notes and spending time together outside of the study group.

But after a month, I felt overwhelmed at living a dual life. At the end of a study session, I pulled Michelle aside and told her I needed to come clean with Tricia.

"I don't want any drama," Michelle said. She looked concerned—afraid, even.

When I got home, Johnny was asleep. "Your dinner's in the oven," Tricia said quietly, not looking up from her magazine. "I hope it's not dried out."

I said, "I need to talk with you."

I sat down next to Tricia on the couch. Her eyes narrowed as she searched my face for clues.

"Listen," I said, hurrying to get the words out. "I've fallen in love with Michelle."

Tricia's fists clenched. She punched the couch cushion and stalked into our bedroom, shutting the door. I followed her and tried the doorknob: locked. I heard her crying.

"Tricia?" I said.

"Fuck you!" she shouted. In his nursery, Johnny started to wail in his crib. I went in and tried to comfort him, but Tricia came out and kept on yelling—yelling and crying. "Selfish son of a bitch!" she screamed. "The only person you care about is you." She took Johnny from my arms and locked me out of the bedroom again.

The next day in class, Michelle avoided my eyes. When I tried to talk to her at lunch, she pulled away. When I reached out again, confused, she turned to face me. "She called me."

"What did she say?" I asked, dreading the answer.

Michelle just shook her head. "I told you," she said. "No drama. You need to figure out who you want to be with. Make a decision: I'm not going to be caught in the middle."

When I got home, Tricia was gone. She'd taken Johnny with her, of course. I stared down at his empty crib as sorrow and guilt spread through my stomach.

That night my mother called. "I can't believe you," she said, her voice full of disgust. Tricia had told everybody what I'd done.

I felt like I was being tortured. Looking down at Johnny's empty crib, filled with worry I'd never see my son again, feeling like a bad, bad guy, I felt desperate to fix this. Without thinking it through, I drove to Buffalo, went to see Tricia, and asked her to take a walk with me. Fumbling for words, I promised I'd do everything I could to make our marriage work. Inside, all I could think was *I need my son back. I have to have the baby back in my house, in my arms, in my life.*

"I will not be fooled around on," she said.

"I won't fool around on you," I said. And I meant it.

But when Tricia brought Johnny back to Wilkes-Barre, within a few weeks I was right back where I'd been before. I wanted to honor my promise to Tricia, but now that I was past the initial pain and fear of losing my son, I wondered: Where would it end? Would the rest of my life be like this, playing out a charade marriage? I felt caught, trapped.

And of course, every time I saw Michelle in class, I felt my heart race. *There's something here. I don't know if it's love—it's too early to tell—but I feel* alive *when I'm around* her.

But after class, as I walked away from campus, my heart and my steps both grew heavier the closer I got to home. *What am I even doing? I know I don't love Tricia. I should, but I never have, and I don't now.* At home, only Johnny brought me joy. The rest of my home life was cold silence, careful politeness, and pain.

So in the end, I broke that promise, a promise I never should have made. I gradually resumed my relationship with Michelle, seeing her and writing her letters.

Was I intentionally careless, on some level wanting Tricia to discover what was going on? I must have been. She found a letter in the trash. She took Johnny and left.

That evening, I came home to an empty house. In the middle of the living room floor lay a crumpled love letter from Michelle, carefully smoothed out and left where I would see it. I picked it up. I wandered into what had been Johnny's room. He wasn't there, of course. Even the crib was gone. I slid to the floor in the dusty outline where the crib had stood, as crumpled as that letter.

Tricia filed for divorce. She was understandably angry, but she showed a big heart—bigger than I could have, I think. She agreed to let me have Johnny on weekends. So every Friday when classes were done, I made the five-hour drive to Buffalo. I'd pick him up from Tricia and take him to my mom's house. Mom still thought I was a real shit for cheating on Tricia, but she was warmed by the way I cared for Johnny. I think it was as fun a time for her as it was for me. He was now more than a year old, and I adored him. I'd let him sleep in bed with me, cuddling him through the night. During the day, we did father-son stuff—fishing, coloring, or our big thing: playing t-ball with a jumbo plastic bat and ball. Sometimes we'd go to the zoo or the playground. I loved those times with Johnny, and I hated having to drop him off at noon on Sundays and then make the lonely five-hour drive back to Wilkes-Barre.

It wasn't an easy time. In addition to needing to study harder than ever, I felt like shit. My house felt empty, missing its heart, without my son. I also felt guilty about what I'd done to Tricia. I can't even begin to imagine how I would have reacted had the roles been reversed. Although I was by now thoroughly estranged from Catholicism, I went to some church counseling sessions; it was what I knew, and at the time, it seemed to help. It was counseling, not Mass. I also found a karate studio with a kickboxing night—another way for me to release stress.

Very early on, I decided I wasn't going to wallow in self-pity. Whenever I started feeling sorry for myself, I'd lace up some roller blades and tear around town until I felt better. And on those drives to and from Buffalo, when I was feeling so down, I listened to educational books on tape, determined to continually improve myself.

Meanwhile, Michelle and I continued to grow closer. She was completely supportive, never complaining when I took off for the weekend to be with Johnny. She knew he was number one in my life at that point.

Even with all of this going on, I made it through the second semester maintaining my high-B average. But our work was only half done. Next, we began a fifteen-month period of intensive six-week rotations, from pediatrics to psychiatry and everything in between at hospitals, doctors' practices, and emergency rooms all over Pennsylvania.

My sense of myself as an imposter had vanished. In fact, I was brimming with confidence. I now knew that, with proper study techniques and my dad's work ethic, I could succeed. And because I'd succeeded in the classroom, I felt prepared clinically. I knew my shit.

My first rotation was at a pediatrics practice. I'll never forget talking with a kid and his mom in the exam room when the doctor—an older man with a long beard—came in. The boy, who'd been calm up to that point, started to freak out. "Oh, the doctor looks like his dad," the mother said.

I noticed bruises on the kid's legs. Instantly, I worried he was being abused. But the doctor ordered some blood work and sent the mom and her child home. I was furious. I stewed for half an hour before knocking at the doctor's door. "I'm concerned about potential child abuse," I said. "I'm worried about what's going to happen when they get home."

The doctor raised his eyebrows. "Let's wait till we get the test results before we start letting our imaginations run wild."

When the lab work came back, it turned out the child's platelet count was low, which accounted for the bruising. The doctor was great about it, even though I must have been near insufferable; here I was, a PA for all of a week, trying to tell this doctor with years of experience that I saw something he couldn't. I was humbled, and I tried to remind myself of that moment whenever I was tempted to think I had all the answers.

During one of my two emergency medicine rotations, I found a dusty foam Batman mask. At the time, Batman was really big. In an effort to make kids feel more at ease, I'd ask them to name their favorite superhero. Inevitably, it was Batman. "You know, I think

I saw him around here," I'd say. "Let me see if I can get him to come in and say hi." I'd leave the room, put on the mask, and return. Kids went crazy. It was a lot of fun.

Of course, it wasn't all fun and games. When I did my surgical rotation, at a small hospital in Dansville, NY, the surgeon asked me whether I'd like to assist on a surgery to repair an aortic aneurism, a serious surgery. I readily agreed.

A few days later, the patient and his wife came in for a pre-surgery visit. An older couple, they sat across from me holding hands. "We're worried," said the wife. "This is such a small hospital, and the operation is so serious, would it make sense for us to transfer to a bigger hospital, even though it's farther from home?"

"That's a great question," I said. "I don't know the answer—but let's ask the surgeon."

When I brought the surgeon in, he was all reassurance. "I do operations like this all the time, right here at this hospital. You don't need to worry for a moment."

Then why have you been bragging about this surgery for days, I wondered. But I was just there to learn.

The day of the operation came. I was a "third assist" behind two surgeons—present and sterile, but basically just there to learn and help out. At six a.m., the patient was put to sleep and intubated, and we began what should have been a four-hour surgery. By eight a.m., all was going well.

Then a small complication: one of the blood vessels burst.

Then another vessel burst. The surgeon cursed softly under his breath.

Next thing I know, it was noon, six hours in, and both surgeons had their hands in the patient, suturing fast, muttering urgent comments to each other.

Then we were seven hours in. Then eight.

And all of a sudden, the patient was bleeding everywhere. His body was shutting down, rejecting this graft.

At ten hours in, the man died on the table. Died right in front of us.

Ripping off our masks and gloves, we staggered out. I will never forget walking out of that operating room: instantly, staff in the post-op area could see what had happened. They stared at me in silence as I walked past, as if to say, *You just went through hell.* Ten hours of standing by the side of a critical patient—no meals, no bathroom breaks—and then to watch him die.

After I washed up, I headed out to the cafeteria to get a cup of coffee. Down the hall, from a distance, I saw the surgeon approach the patient's wife. Watched him tell her. Watched her break down.

I was "just there to learn," and I learned more than I bargained for. It was a good lesson for someone like me, who tends to be cocky and take risks. But I got that lesson at a pretty terrible cost.

Despite that incident, and the rigorous schedule, and the inevitable ups and downs, I loved the work. Interacting with patients, doctors, and nurses was a blast. I excelled in my rotations. I didn't even mind living out of a suitcase for six weeks at a time. Because the rotations were at spots throughout Pennsylvania and New York, I had to find short-term living arrangements. For one rotation, I stayed at a bed-and-breakfast. For another, I lived in an extended-stay motel until I got into a beef with management about how noisy the place was. I finally decided to stay at the duplex in Wilkes-Barre for the remainder of that rotation, even though it meant more than an hour commute both ways.

No matter where I was, I went home every weekend to be with Johnny. Because our time together was precious, I was determined to be proactive in planning out activities: we weren't going to sit around and watch TV. I'll never forget taking him to fish at a little trout stream before he could even talk. I taught him how to cast his bright red-and-blue Fisher-Price rod into the gurgling water. The line tugged gently, so I put my arms around him, holding the pole, and pulled in a small, brown trout. I held it up for Johnny to see it—I was certain it was the first fish he'd ever seen out of water—and his eyes got wide with curiosity. But just as he got close, the fish started flopping on the line. Johnny's eyes widened even more and he started pointing wildly at the water; he wanted me to get the fish back in the stream, and fast.

Through it all, Michelle and I continued to grow closer, even though we were long distance a lot of the time. We spent time together when we could, taking long walks or going rollerblading. And we talked. Michelle had lived a relatively protected life, so she was fascinated with my more unconventional experiences. She liked hearing about my time in the Marines, the fights I got into, my struggles in school.

Meanwhile, my relationship with my parents seemed to smooth out—no doubt because I was a little more mature, and generally happy. Although Dad never became warm and fuzzy, he showed his care in other ways. When I had an OB-GYN rotation in the Buffalo area, I stayed with him. Sometimes we'd play chess, though I'd gotten pretty good at it in the Marines, and Dad still didn't like to lose.

I continued to stay with Mom when I'd come in for weekends with Johnny. She really seemed to enjoy herself with a baby in the house, and she was always fussing over Johnny when I didn't have him occupied. It was good to see her smile again.

But my interactions with Tricia remained strained. At one point, we landed in court because she claimed she wasn't getting enough support for Johnny. I initially gave her cash, but quickly came to realize that cash left no record of itself. So I started paying her with money orders and grocery store gift cards. The court quickly dismissed her claim once my lawyer produced a sheaf of receipts.

The only time she really enraged me was on Halloween, when she claimed Johnny was sick and couldn't come trick-or-treating with me as planned. I had been looking forward to this for weeks, and her refusal to let me have him infuriated me. I insisted on seeing Johnny to see whether he was really sick. He wasn't—he was perfectly fine, and Tricia was just trying to hurt me by withholding my son.

But over the next year, things slowly got a bit better between us. The day before our divorce was final, Tricia called. "You sure you want to go through with this?" she asked.

I stared at the phone in my hand. *Is she crazy?* "What the fuck?"

She laughed. "Just kidding," she said.

My final rotation was a six-month stint at a family practice in Hamburg. I stayed with Dad again, and we resumed our cool but cordial relations. He showed his care and support not with hugs or deep talks, but with money. During my second year of PA school, I was having trouble making ends meet, so at the beginning of the school year, Dad had loaned me $10,000 at a modest interest rate. That spring, as graduation was drawing near, Dad said to me, "That $10,000, it's a gift. You don't have to worry about paying it back." His only condition: I wasn't to tell my mom what he'd done—which was weird, because she seemed to resent that Dad hadn't helped me financially earlier in my schooling.

Having that loan forgiven helped a lot, but I was still concerned about what I'd do after graduation. I desperately wanted to be in the Buffalo area so I could be close to Johnny, but I wasn't finding anything. I initially accepted a job with a cardiology practice in Schenectady, New York, after they put me up in a swank hotel and offered me an amazing salary and benefits. But my gut told me it was the wrong thing to do. I knew I would only leave as soon as I found something else in Buffalo. So I backed out. Shortly after that, I was offered an ER job in Buffalo.

It was a great feeling to head into graduation with a job in hand. Michelle still hadn't found a

Buffalo-area job, which concerned me. We both knew we would stay together no matter what, but I sensed that our relationship would suffer if she wasn't working in Buffalo, too. Still, I felt a sense of optimism. As my classmates and I gathered back in Wilkes-Barre for graduation, I decided we all deserved a party—a grown-up affair at a hotel conference hall, with a DJ and dinner and dancing, something where we would all dress up. Michelle liked the idea, but she was doubtful that very many people would show up. It turned out almost *everybody* showed up, bringing friends and family, eager to celebrate and have fun as a group.

At the party, we even had our own little awards ceremony. I was proud to be named "Most Motivated PA"—especially with my dad and Billy in the audience. In the beginning, back when I'd been so convinced I was an imposter, I'd vowed to outwork everyone. My classmates had noticed. I felt so proud and gratified not only to have succeeded, but to have been seen for who I truly was.

It was a beautiful night. We got instructors and Dr. Babonis, the program director, to speak; one of my favorite professors, Dr. Robert Czwalina, even made a reference to a sort of inside joke of ours from class.

During a lecture, three times within a couple of minutes he'd used the word "serendipity." I had to raise my hand and ask what that word meant. It seemed like a key point, and I wanted to make sure I understood. He defined the word, but first he lit into me. "This is a graduate program," he thundered, "and you don't know what the word 'serendipity' means?"

A little later, he had trouble with the classroom projector. Being a wiseass, I said something like, "That projector is being serendipitous."

He countered: "I'll be serendipitous with your grade."

In his speech, Dr. Czwalina mentioned the episode, noting how it made us all laugh. But then he said, "Make sure you enjoy the serendipity of this profession. Don't miss the beauty." That really stuck with me. I quote it to this day.

As the evening progressed, I felt great joy and also great caution. Big questions rose in my mind. How would I pay back the $100,000 in student loans it had taken to get me to this point? And I wondered— looking at Michelle laughing and raising her glass of champagne—what did the future hold for us?

Chapter 8

Before the Fall

Limos, flashing lights, glitz: I got a taste of what it would be like to be a big shot when my dad took me to Las Vegas as a graduation present. But the trip wasn't all. He gave me a card, writing inside that he was proud of me and enclosing four checks for one hundred dollars each—gambling money, a check for each day of our trip.

Dad had arranged a large credit line with the casino in advance, so we were treated like royalty. We got picked up at the airport in a shiny black limo, and the casino comped us a deluxe suite. We even got free tickets for a comedy show—front-row center seats. It was glamour like I'd never experienced before.

The first day, I was wide-eyed walking through the windowless casino, absorbing the amiable patter of the craps table stickmen ("Six with ease like spaghetti and cheese!"), the blinking lights of the slot machines, and the overwhelming feeling of being surrounded by wealth: the polished marble columns, gold crown molding, and piles of chips everywhere.

I lost one hundred dollars.

The second day, though, I caught fire at the craps table, winning $1,800 for the day. Knowing that I would almost certainly lose it all back, I found a little bank, got a cashier's check for $1,600, and mailed it to myself. No matter what else happened over the next two days, I would have that money waiting for me when I got home.

"Johnny, you didn't need to do that," Dad said. "You could have given it to me and I'd have kept it for you."

"I know," I said. "But I also know you would have given it back to me if I'd asked so that I could gamble more. This way I know it's safe."

He kept giving me a hard time about it that night, but the next day I heard him bragging on me. "My son's a smart one," he told a fellow gambler. "He's going home a winner."

The Vegas trip was a cool and exciting experience for me, but I didn't buy into the façade of it all. The glamour and feel of being a big shot were seductive, but I also knew it was a mirage. I saw plenty of sad people there who had bought into the fantasy and suffered for it.

When we returned to Buffalo, I faced a slow adjustment to my new life. It still took a month or so for all the paperwork and certification to get processed for my new job in the ER. The good news for me was that Michelle had also finally landed a job in Buffalo—a position with a small, inner-city practice. She got a place in a really nice, professional apartment complex about twenty-five minutes away from my Dad's house, where I was still living—an easy drive.

When I finally got to start working in the late fall of 1997, I was determined to kick ass and be a productive PA. My mindset was that I was going to *dominate* emergency medicine. I was enthusiastic and excited to share everything I'd learned in PA school—to really help people and shake up the status quo.

During one of our many long talks during this period, Michelle and I playfully explored what I considered one of the most important questions in our line of work: what was more important, confidence or competence?

Michelle chose competence every time. "We're dealing with people's lives and health," she said. "You have to know what you're doing."

"You're wrong," I replied. "If you have a façade, if you carry yourself with the air of knowing what you're doing, patients will trust you and do what you say. It's a lot more important to have confidence."

And that's the attitude I carried. Sure, I wanted to be competent. But more than anything, I wanted to be a hero, to be the guy who saved the day, saved the leg, saved the life. That was my way of being a big shot. In the ER, even if there were more than enough cases for everyone on duty, I would scoop up an armful of charts, ensuring I'd see the most patients—ensuring I'd be the star. I wanted to impress people, and I wanted to prove myself. And for the most part, I was acing it. At least, so I thought.

But the head PA, Jill, always rubbed me the wrong way. Because she had worked at the hospital as a nurse before becoming a PA, she was friendly with the nurses. And yet she was constantly sneaking around behind their backs: "I'm going to do this, but don't tell the nurses." Or "Don't tell the nurse I said this." It felt duplicitous to me.

After a while, Jill seemed to develop a vendetta against me. Because I was so intent on maximizing efficiency—and because I was still a fairly new PA, learning on the job—I sometimes made careless mistakes or missed things. The way Jill criticized me didn't make me want to learn and grow—it made me defensive and resentful.

One time a patient came in complaining of urinary symptoms: the patient had to urinate frequently, and it burned. I ordered some tests, but instead of waiting for the results—which would have meant that sick and injured patients sitting in the waiting room had to wait even longer—I sent the patient home with an antibiotic. I went on to the next case, feeling as though I'd done an efficient job of keeping the ER moving.

It wasn't long before I heard from Jill. "Test came back on your urinary tract patient," she said with thinly-veiled glee. "You made a mistake. The antibiotic you prescribed won't do a thing for this infection." Knowing what was coming, I just stayed silent, waiting for her to keep bashing me. Sure enough, she continued scolding: "You should have waited for the results and given a different drug. Now we have to track the patient down."

Jill was constantly wagging a finger and rubbing my nose in my rookie mistakes. Whenever she called me at home, I would instantly get a knot in my stomach. But when she called me out in front of my peers, it just pissed me off and made me defensive. *I'll show her*, I'd think. I resented being ordered around or treated like I was inferior—I figured we were all in this game of patient care together, and we should treat each other as equals. That's how I tried to treat everyone, from the orderlies right up to the hospital's most powerful VIPs.

I still believe in treating people as equals. But what didn't occur to me then was that I was coming across as an arrogant ass. A guy just out of school should show some humility and admit his mistakes, instead of being angry at the person who pointed them out, however tactlessly.

Here's another example of me in arrogant ass mode—it was the first time I met Dr. Platte, a powerful, well-known cardiologist. Around the ER, he was the man, and when he walked into a room, he owned it. The first time he saw me, he greeted me amiably: "Well, hi. So you're the new PA."

"I'm not a PA," I replied, with just a touch of snark, "but I do play one on TV." His pleasant expression shifted into a frown. *Sorry, doc*, I thought, *but I want you to know who you're dealing with—I'm not going to kiss your feet just because of your reputation.*

There was another doc named Dr. Rossi. Unlike Dr. Platte, Dr. Rossi wasn't well liked. He was a sour, pissed-off guy who often referred to our patients as scumbags. I couldn't believe how dismissive he was, how derogatory. Finally I felt I had to speak up. "These people aren't *scumbags*," I said. "I don't feel that way at all."

Maybe it was because of that comment, or maybe because of my general arrogance, but after that, he started being a real dick to me. One day I was supposed to get off work at ten p.m., but I found myself handling a steady stream of patients on my own while Dr. Rossi sat and read the newspaper. Even after I was done seeing these patients, I still had another half hour of work filling out patient charts, so I was already going to be working past quitting time.

There was one patient left. "Hey," Dr. Rossi said, flipping a page of the paper, not looking up. "After you see this last patient, you can go."

I should have agreed with a smile; after all, I was the one who wanted to be the hero, and I was low down in the pecking order. Instead, I threw a hissy fit.

"No," I said. "I've got three charts I have to do. I'm not going to see your patient."

He picked up that patient's chart and threw it at me. "Too fucking bad."

I threw it back at him. "You're seeing him."

He tossed his newspaper onto the desk, grabbed the chart, and stormed off to see the patient. *Not sure that was smart*, said a small voice in the back of my head—but I shook it off. I may have been the new guy, but the way I saw it, no one was going to walk all over me—not even a doctor.

As I tried to make my mark, I was determined to prove my worth and show everyone that I knew my medicine. Again, that sometimes made me a lousy coworker. One day Dr. Colin McMahon, a doctor I liked and admired, said that if any kids came in with fevers of 103 degrees or more, he wanted to make sure we did blood cultures. Instead of just agreeing to do it because he was the doctor, I asked to see for myself the studies that showed that was the right thing to do. He was appropriately annoyed.

Another time, Dr. McMahon made a generic statement about how ectopic pregnancies don't cause vaginal bleeding. Well, I'd seen it happen earlier that same week; we'd had to rush the woman to the operating room. So I challenged him. "Yes they do," I said.

"No, they bleed into their bellies."

I'd been a PA for six months, and he was a board-certified internal medicine and pediatrics physician. He was a super-smart guy. But none of that meant he was right all the time—I was right and I knew it. That's fair—but unfortunately, I wanted everyone else to know it, too. I continued to argue with him back and forth until finally I grabbed an emergency medicine book.

"Ectopic pregnancies do three things," I read. "They cause right lower quadrant pain, a missed period, and vaginal bleeding."

I set the book down and pointed to the passage. Dr. McMahon glanced at it, closed the book, and stormed out. "The book is wrong," he said over his shoulder. He didn't sound happy.

But I was happy. *I showed you! This PA is on fire!*

Anyway, that's what I thought at the time.

Just as I was always ready to prove my knowledge, I was also ready to come to the defense of anyone I thought needed it. It wasn't so much that I saw myself as an avenging superhero; I just had an elevated sense of the way people should be treated—and of myself. What I lacked was humility and the good sense of knowing what battles to engage in.

I once caught a charge nurse really ripping into a resident, bullying her brutally in front of all the other nurses. The resident looked like she was about to cry. I'd seen this same nurse pull this kind of abuse before, and it always made me angry. This time, I said something.

"You know what you should do?" I said to the nurse. "You should go to nurse practitioner school. You're so smart, they may waive all your classes and just give you a degree. And once you're a nurse practitioner, your medical opinion will actually be relevant." I paused, letting the cutting remark sink in. "But as of now, you don't have that degree, so you don't really have a medical opinion that's relevant."

Boy, was she pissed—but if she was going to make other people feel so bad and demoralized, I thought she should be ready to take some of her own medicine. What I didn't see was my own growing pattern of arrogant smart-mouthing.

Another time, I insulted a longtime ER secretary. She was always leaving the ER on some fake errand so she could smoke. A lot of times she'd say she was going on a coffee run and offer to bring back drinks for others, but she'd be gone for big chunks of time. I found it annoying and inconvenient, and I told her so. "When you work, my job is harder because you're never at your desk," I said. She cried.

Dr. McMahon pulled me aside. He gave me a slightly admonishing frown, but he followed it with a wink: "How dare you tell her what everybody is thinking?" he said.

If the rest of them were thinking it, I wondered, *how come nobody said anything to her?* The way I saw it at the time, I was standing up for everyone whose life she was making more difficult. What I didn't see was that I had just made a coworker cry—just like that charge nurse.

Aside from my run-ins with coworkers, I was working my ass off. I arrived to work early. I stayed late. I saw tons of patients. I was trying to be a great PA. I was pulling more than my weight, and I was proving that I knew medicine. As I saw it, sure, some of my colleagues needed to be set right once in a while, but this was a small price to pay to get to live out my dream.

As I was proving myself in the ER, things were also going well with Michelle. I spent more and more nights at her place for the first six months we were both working, and then I just moved in with her. The apartment complex was nice and upscale, filled mostly with older professionals. We were the young couple, and the world looked good.

So almost a year after graduation, in the fall of 1998, I was having the occasional hiccup at work, but overall I was doing what I had set out to do. Meanwhile, Michelle—after having issues with her own first job— had landed a new position with a practice where she's remained ever since.

And then, just before Christmas 1998, the rug was yanked from under my feet.

On a cold morning in early December, as I stood in the ER, brushing sleet off my coat, an intake nurse told me I was to report to Dr. John Brock's office. I'd always gotten along well with Dr. Brock, who ran the ER—but when I arrived to find him accompanied by Jill and the nursing manager, I had a queasy feeling. *Damn. Did I make another mistake? I can't think of anything I did wrong. I've been super-strong on my clinical medicine. Hell, maybe they're giving me a promotion.*

"John," Dr. Brock began. "We want you to find a new job."

I looked from his face to Jill's; I swear she was smirking.

Dr. Brock continued: "If you go quietly, we'll give you good references. If you are loud and make it hard for us, we're going to make it hard on you."

For a moment I couldn't say a word. Finally I managed to say, "I understand. I'll put in my thirty-day notice."

When I left Dr. Brock's office, I felt dazed. *How did this happen? What am I going to do?*

I saw Dr. McMahon. I tried to collect myself. "I just got fired," I told him, my voice laced with disbelief.

He put a sympathetic hand on my shoulder. "John," he said gently, "you're not easy to work with."

All at once, flash cuts of my fifteen months at the ER raced through my mind—my resistance to criticism, my showboating, my confrontational attitude. My arrogance—I'd been so full of shit. Then I thought about all the hard work I had done, all the good I had done. Didn't those count for more? It didn't seem like it.

Dr. McMahon, Dr. Brock, and Jill were all telling me, in so many words, that I wasn't worth all the bullshit.

Michelle was kind and sympathetic, trying to ease my hurt, but it didn't help. I remember going over to Dad's and slumping on his couch, hanging my head. He tried bucking me up. "It's your first job, Johnny," he said. "Better things are to come." I didn't believe him.

As I served out the last month of my job, I quieted down and made no waves. That month was the worst. No one said anything to me, but I knew everyone else knew I'd been fired. I was humiliated, ashamed, and angry. On my last day of work, I had to leave early—which was unheard of for me—because I was sick with a fever and an upset stomach. I have no doubt my illness was the result of my embarrassment, anxiety, and stress.

On some level, I recognized that I hadn't understood the politics of the ER, hadn't known how to play the game. But it would be a very long time before I saw how much ego I'd had—how wrong I'd been to act the way I did. Needlessly being a jerk to Dr. Platte. Pointlessly challenging Dr. McMahon. Throwing my weight around with the charge nurse—basically doing to her what I thought she was doing to the residents—and to what purpose?

Left with nothing but hours to think about my situation, my mind spiraled. *Will I be labeled a problem PA? Will I get blackballed? I'm such a fool.* I moped and spent lots of my time on the couch.

It was the beginning of a brand-new year, 1999, but I felt like the future was bleak. Michelle tried her best to help me, but she couldn't quite find the words. So one morning as she left for work while I sulked on the couch, she set a box on the coffee table in front of me.

"Maybe this will help," she said. It was a movie: *Rudy*. I smiled. It was a beautiful gesture.

Fortunately, my fears that my dreams had been dashed were unfounded. True to his word, Dr. Brock provided me with a great reference, and in less than a month, I was hired in an exciting and challenging position: a hospitalist PA. I was to manage those patients who were ill enough to be in the hospital, yet not in the intensive care unit. As excited as I was about the job in a new hospital, I entered with some apprehension. Would my new boss be like Jill? Would I continue to have run-ins with doctors?

I shouldn't have worried. My new boss, John Caven, was absolutely awesome. If I made a mistake, he'd quietly take me aside.

"So what did you see when you met with this patient?" he'd ask—gently, so I didn't get defensive. "Tell me what went through your mind."

As I explained, he would nod patiently. "Oh, I see," he'd say. "But when I see that, it makes me think about …" He was a masterful teacher, helping me discover my own errors. I owe a great deal of my success in medicine to John Caven.

This job as a hospitalist was a sixty-minute drive each way. I took advantage of this. I would listen to audiobooks all the time about medicine, leadership, and human interactions.

At my first job, my attitude had been *Fuck you guys—you don't know what I know. I'm connecting the dots in ways you don't see.* That was my delusion: *I'm smarter than everyone.* I'd pretend what I did was for the greater good, but it was always about me. I wanted to climb the ladder of success, and I didn't care who I was stepping on, who I disrespected.

After I got fired—not right away, but eventually—I had an epiphany: *You fucked up, John. This is on you.* That's why I was listening to audiobooks on relationships, books by Dale Carnegie, Stephen Covey, Anthony Robbins, and others. I never wanted to be in a position again where I would get fired for intrapersonal issues.

Whether this was a deep core change, or whether I was just fine-tuning my façade—that remained to be seen.

As I settled into my new job, learning and growing as a PA under John's wise guidance, Michelle and I got our own place, a nicely furnished apartment on top of a garage. To me, the best thing about the carriage house was that it was *ours*. I was happy to come home to this place we'd picked out together. And I loved what it represented: the deepening of our commitment to each other. Even though we now saw each other every day, we still had long talks, and Michelle was as ready as ever to bring me down to earth. Once I found six hundred dollars in cash, lying on the ground. I was so thrilled—didn't give a thought to whoever might have dropped it, didn't wait to see if they'd come back looking, didn't check around. Just gave a hundred to Billy and pocketed the rest. "Check it out!" I said to Michelle when I came home that night. I landed beside her on the couch, pulling the roll out of my front pocket. "Found this on the ground! Lucky day or what? Maybe we could ..." I stopped. Michelle's face didn't look right. She looked worried.

She marked her place in her book and closed it. "Couldn't you find the owner?"

"Well," I said, feeling suddenly uneasy. "I mean, I didn't really try. That kind of cash, you know, it's probably a drug dealer, or something."

A long silence. Then, not quite looking at me, she said, "... yeah. Maybe a drug dealer. Or maybe a guy who does lawns, who just collected a whole week's pay, and won't be able to make rent next month."

She was right, and I knew it. I'd only thought of my own good luck, and not the other's guy's bad luck. I felt ashamed.

As Christmas of 1999 approached, I marveled at how much better things were this year than they'd been the year before. I'd been so down and out, convinced that everything I had worked so hard for was ruined. Now, I was right where I was supposed to be. When you're in the middle of a shitty situation, you can't see the blessings. But now that my life was back on track, I saw what a gift I'd been given by being fired. It was a reality check. If I hadn't gotten fired, I'd have continued being an ass to doctors, nurses, and staff. I remembered Dr. McMahon's observation that I was difficult to work with. Losing my job helped me grow as a person. And now, I was growing as a practitioner.

One night, Michelle excused herself after dinner to take a bubble bath. I waited for her to fill the tub, and then waited a little longer for her to get settled. I knocked at the door and entered before she could reply. I dropped to a knee. "Michelle, you deserve the very best," I said as she brought her soap-bubbled hands to her face. "But I hope you'll agree to marry me anyway."

She let out a quick sob and embraced me in a soapy hug.

We immediately began thinking about starting a family together. Michelle had told me that she was concerned about having endometriosis; she was worried she might not be able to have children. She knew I could have no relationship at all with my first son, Corey, and never even heard from Tina about him. She also knew how much it hurt me that I couldn't be a full-time dad for Johnny. And she also knew I'd love to raise a family with her. "You know," she said, "we probably shouldn't wait until the wedding to start trying for a family. It might take a while." So we started trying right away.

That Christmas Eve, I watched quietly, sipping a beer, as Michelle and Johnny decorated the tree. I smiled as Michelle talked to Johnny about Santa Claus while they hung ornaments. When Johnny went to bed, I got a paper bag and made a cutout template of a boot track, sprinkling flour through the boot-shaped hole to make "Santa tracks" into the house for Johnny to find in the morning. I even made tracks into the bathroom, suggesting a post-delivery pee break for Santa. Johnny and I had tied a carrot to a rope and flung it onto the roof, a snack for the reindeer. I replaced the carrot with a half-eaten one so Johnny would be convinced that Rudolph had taken the bait. As I saw Johnny's face light up, I remembered the way Mom had made Christmas magical for me when I was little.

My life was full—and it was about to get even fuller. Just one month after we started trying, Michelle was pregnant. I was going to get to be a full-time dad. My life just kept getting better and better.

Michelle and I married at Saint Gregory the Great, a Roman Catholic Church in Buffalo, on April 29, 2000—one of the best days of my life. I can still see Johnny, my ring bearer, holding the pillow with the ring high as he walked down the aisle, a grin spread across his whole face. I held back tears. Michelle was stunning. The love I felt in her sparkling brown eyes filled me with joy. I was floating.

Our reception at the Glen Oak, a Buffalo golf course and country club, was raucous and joyful, with our guests singing along to songs like "Paradise by the Dashboard Light" and "Summer Lovin'." I avoided looking at my mom, who was still determined to be angry with my dad and ignore him. I wasn't going to let anything rain on my parade. It was a wonderful day.

Once we came back to earth, we began preparing for the birth of our son. On November 1, 2000, Michelle's water broke. At first, everything was moving along fine. The obstetrician checked on us and said everything was progressing as it should, but it would be hours before the delivery. Michelle and I chatted between her contractions.

Suddenly, the fetal heart monitor sounded an alarm: the baby's heart rate had slowed significantly.

It was a sign of fetal distress, probably caused either by a prolapsed umbilical cord or from the cord being wrapped around his neck. Nurses rushed in, and I felt a wave of panic. *This can't be happening. Everything was fine.*

Being a medical practitioner, and knowing what

was happening, only made things worse. I read the fear in the nurses' faces. I knew what could happen in the worst-case scenario: cerebral palsy, death. Time slowed down. I stared down at my wife, not even trying to mask my terror. She was on pain medication, foggy and confused. They wheeled her into surgery for an emergency C-section, and I felt like I'd been dropped into the ocean. All my PA training was no help to me— if anything, it made things worse. I knew my child was not getting oxygen, and I knew just how bad that could be. And yet I had no control, no way of helping, no way of being a hero. I couldn't even follow Michelle into the operating room.

I had no idea how long it took for the doctor to arrive, for them to finally take her into the operating room. I'd guess that from the time the fetal monitor went off to the time they had the baby out and breathing, maybe twenty minutes. That's unbelievably fast. I was ushered into the operating room in time to see my son born. Matthew Bielinski was healthy, and Michelle was okay. We were blessed. The doctors and nurses had saved the day, and I felt, more than ever, the weight and beauty of practicing medicine. I understood better than ever how, in my role as a PA, I could be the miracle worker for others.

Johnny came to the hospital to meet his baby brother. He looked like an angel, eyes wide with wonder, peering into Matthew's tiny, scrunched-up face. I felt so blessed in that moment.

Of course, once we got Matthew home, I often felt helpless and useless. When Matthew cried in the middle of the night, I'd get up and try to calm him—but I just couldn't soothe him. He was hungry, and because Michelle was breastfeeding, I was of no help. What I could do was be a strong provider, and that fit into my mindset of what made a good father. I was the hunter, the gatherer, the family protector.

So when I got another opportunity to provide more for my family, I took it. Buffalo had two PA schools then—one with a very strong reputation, and the other a Catholic college, D'Youville, that was still developing its program. D'Youville called me and said they needed a lab medicine teacher.

I said I would think about it. I had reservations. "I don't know how to teach lab medicine!" I said to John Craven, my boss.

He nodded at me. "You're taking care of very sick people here in the hospital," he said. "Just go and teach them clinical medicine. Don't worry about getting academic on them. Just teach them what you do every day."

I'd long been attracted to the idea of teaching—I remembered the excitement and warmth I'd felt when some memory trick I came up with helped the Johnny's Angels group learn difficult material—and I'd been an instructor in advanced cardiac life support for a local ambulance company. But this would be my first experience standing in front of forty students I'd be with for a full semester.

When I accepted the job, they delivered a thick binder of the previous teacher's slides. I looked through them with increasing disgust: it was all purely academic, the kind of stuff you see in textbooks, not in the real world. So I put them aside and never looked at them again. "I want to teach the class my way," I told the administrators. They said that was fine, and I took them at their word.

As I prepared, I thought back to my second-grade teacher, Mr. Black. I wanted to be like Mr. Black: tough yet fair, guiding students to do the best they could through creative learning that challenged the status quo.

I taught my first class in January 2001. I went there straight from work, wearing my scrubs. As I stood in front of the class—young people lined up in rows of desks, notebooks open to blank pages, looking at me expectantly—I felt a wave of nerves. But I just started talking: first introducing myself and then explaining what I hoped to accomplish during the semester. The nerves disappeared.

I strove to be like Mr. Black, with high standards but individual kindness—and above all, to prepare the students to be effective PAs. During the first ten minutes of every class, from 8:00–8:10 a.m., I gave a ten-point, fill-in-the-blanks quiz. The quizzes were cumulative, so even on the last day, I might have a question from the first day of class. I didn't want students just cramming; I wanted them to have a deep understanding of medicine. Every day the quiz was closed at the end of ten minutes. If a student was delayed by traffic, too bad. "You have to allow extra time for the unexpected," I said. "If you're assisting a surgeon, you better not be late, and this is as good a time to learn that as any."

"I got other classes, you know," a young man grumbled one morning as he swung his backpack over one sweatshirted shoulder after class.

Stone-faced, I listened.

He ran his hands through brown curls in frustration. "C'mon, Mr. B., I hate having to study every single night for this one class."

I slipped my notes in my own backpack. "Would you prefer not knowing critical information?"

He paused, then the scowl disappeared, replaced by a grin. "Nah," he said. "I love that part. We *are* gonna be badasses, that's for sure. But damn, you're making us work for it!"

Most of my students seemed to have that love-hate relationship with me: they hated me because they had to study all the time, but they loved knowing their stuff. One of my students was an older man who had been a physician in Ukraine. I'd heard he was a terror to the other instructors because he knew more than they did. He wasn't a terror to me. He told me one day that he loved my class because I taught him real-life knowledge. I was teaching from my experience.

I was passionate about teaching and found it came naturally to me. I went in and taught them what they needed to know and helped them memorize it the same way I had—with mnemonics.

I was never content, though, always wondering how I could get better. I wanted to find out how I could deliver the material with greater impact. Should I tell a story, or should I use a joke? I was willing to do anything to get better as a teacher. At the end of the semester, I got great evaluations, and the school ended up offering me more teaching jobs.

I was a successful PA with my dream job, helping people, being their miracle. I had a beautiful wife and two beautiful sons. I was a respected, successful teacher. I felt like I owned the world.

My ego was strong—and soon it would be stronger than I was.

Chapter 9

Mission: Control

One day, stepping out of the shower, I caught a glimpse of my body in the mirror. *Is that me?* I was not impressed—after PA school, I realized, I had let myself go. I was almost thirty-three now, and I knew I had to get back in shape.

I decided to learn Krav Maga, an Israeli self-defense system—hardcore and real badass. It didn't take long for me to round into shape, and it took even less time for my kickboxing experience to show. Not long after I'd begun lessons, I was asked to step in and spar with anyone who was getting too rough. No problem. I enjoyed teaching people lessons. I became a kind of enforcer at the gym.

Within a year—in the fall of 2001—I was working as an instructor at the studio, teaching classes after getting off the night shift at the hospital. Just like at the hospital and in the classroom, I was a no-nonsense instructor on the mat. When I was teaching, you'd better be paying attention. One morning, I was demonstrating some moves to use if an attacker approaches with a knife.

One of the students walked onto the mat in the middle of my demonstration. "You have to see what's on TV," he said.

You're interrupting my class to talk about TV? "Get the fuck off my mat!" I barked.

The student shook his head slowly, his eyes frightened. "You don't understand," he said. "Come and see."

We walked into the lobby and stared at the television; my jaw dropped. Smoke billowed from one of the World Trade Center towers. Along with most of America on September 11, 2001, I watched, transfixed and horrified. I looked over my shoulder at the students. "We're done for the day."

Then, as we watched, a second plane flew directly into the second tower. I was chilled to the bone, numb—and scared. *Holy shit. Is the country under attack?* Of course, my reaction was hardly unique. Anyone who witnessed the towers fall that day can recall what they were doing at the time and how they felt. But I knew one thing: no one was going to catch me with my guard down. On my way home, I stopped at a hunting store to buy a lock-blade hunting knife. I was going to be ready for anything.

Michelle was at work when I got home, and Matthew was at daycare. I had a fitful nap, and when I woke up, I thought maybe it had all been a nightmare. But when I flipped on the TV, there it was. One of the reports mentioned a need for medical providers in New York City, so I provided my contact information. Before heading off to work that evening, I prepared a bag in case I got the call. It never came, but I was ready and eager to do what I could.

It's become cliché to say that everything changed on 9/11. And again, I don't want to say that my reactions to that day were special or out of the ordinary. But what is clear to me as I look back on that period is that the terrorist attacks reignited my desire to fight and protect—to be in control of my own fate.

In the weeks that followed, during my Krav Maga instruction, I created scenarios where my students had one shot at taking out a terrorist on a plane. In my own workouts, I visualized bringing down terrorists, protecting my family, defending my country. I understood that the world we were living in was one where warriors were sorely needed, and I believed I could be a warrior once again, given the chance.

Yet everyday life marched on. I was working long hours at the hospital, and I was continuing to build my reputation as a teacher for PA students. Students seemed to love my atypical approach to teaching, which could sometimes be off-color as I tried to make an impression on them and really grab their attention.

One day I came into class after a long shift, stood at the front of the class, and sighed.

"As some of you may know, I hate delivering babies," I began. "Today, we got a call about a woman en route who'd already had five babies. She was going to be delivering as soon as she arrived."

I surveyed the class and saw all the students looking at me intently, some on the edge of their seats.

"The woman arrived, and sure enough, she delivered right away," I continued. "Unfortunately, the baby was microcephalic and he was born without eyelids, so the nurses had to work feverishly to keep his eyes hydrated."

A student gasped, and I heard shocked whispers.

"We sent him off to Children's Hospital, where doctors did something really interesting—they circumcised him and used the foreskin to graft eyelids," I said, shaking my head as I pulled notes out of my backpack. "Long day." I went to the whiteboard to write out a mnemonic.

"How did it turn out?" a student asked.

"Well, he came out a little *cock-eyed*," I said, allowing the words to hang in the air. After a shocked silence, the class roared with laughter.

The students liked me enough that sometimes they invited me out for drinks. And I usually went with them, eroding the distance between student and instructor. When I look back on that, I realize it was a mistake, unprofessional. But at that time, it was validation for my ego. *I walk on water at this school.*

Early in 2002, I went into the school office to check my mail. In the break room, I saw a group of my colleagues clustered around a professor, congratulating her. She'd just been offered a lecturing gig for a national organization.

"How'd you get that?" I asked. To me, she didn't seem like a particularly good instructor—her lectures consisted of her reading off slides in an unbroken monotone.

"I just submitted my lecture and they liked it," she said.

I immediately went to work preparing five lectures to submit to the national governing body. *I've got to be a shoo-in*, I thought. *If she got a deal, there's no way I won't. When I teach, it's like wildfire.* I put a ton of work into my package.

A few weeks later, checking my email, I felt a surge of elation—it was the group I'd submitted to. I opened it eagerly. "Thank you for your kind submission ..." Oh no. The governing body had refused all five. *You guys don't understand*, I thought incredulously. *I'm a good speaker.* What I know now but didn't then was that the topics you propose are more important than how good you may be as a presenter. Frustrated as hell, I didn't want all my hard work to go to waste. So I started sending my package to state organizations with a cover letter asking them to give me a call if they wanted a lecturer. The North Dakota group bit—I was going to Fargo.

My first time on the conference stage had a rough spot or two. That lecture wasn't great to begin with. Then, at one point, I quoted something scientifically divisive. A woman in the audience called out, "Wait a second—what you're saying is pretty controversial. What's your reference?"

Silence. I had one, but I didn't have it on me. I could hear murmurs of disapproval and suspicion in the crowd. Boy, I learned that day: if you're going to quote something controversial to a medical audience, you better have your ammo on you.

"I don't have it on me," I said, hating how weak that sounded. "I'll get it to you after the lecture." And I did.

But it didn't go over well at all. I learned a lesson there.

My next lecture went much better. Something I like to do is start with a big attention-getter, really get people focused. So at the last minute, I altered my opening slides. I said: "Good medicine is based on patient perception—same way speakers are judged. Am I a good speaker? Well, that's based on your perception. I'm going to run an experiment to see if I can read your perception." I could feel the skepticism, but it didn't stop me. "So think of a number 1–10 ..."

And I ran a little "mind-reading" trick on them—I won't explain it here, but you have people think of numbers, letters corresponding to those numbers, then countries and animals, etc., associated with the letters. In the end I revealed my slide, which contained the words everyone in that room had been thinking: "There are no orange kangaroos in Denmark."

The place went fucking crazy. All of a sudden, I had them. For the rest of my presentation they were riveted, and afterward I was mobbed.

So while I made some mistakes in Fargo, I got things right as well. What's more, I wanted to get better. I knew I could dust the other lecturers in their suits, relying on graphs, droning away without even trying to entertain or engage the audience.

I was all *about* the audience, taking people on an emotional roller coaster—just as I was in my community college speech class. I wanted to get them laughing so hard one minute they had tears rolling down their eyes, and then in the next minute relate a story of clinical impact that made audience members understand the gravity of their chosen profession. Being in one of my lectures was like going on an adventure.

Another technique I use, also building off my classroom experience, is what I call active engagement learning. My theory about learning is that right behind the frontal bone in your brain is a secretary who's ready to pull files. If I ask you to name the first person to walk on the moon, the secretary pulls a file—Neil Armstrong.

I believe that it's when that secretary is in the process of pulling files that one gets knowledgeable. Now, literature on adult learning says you need to hear things six times before you'll know it for the rest of your life. So you have to study something, leave it, and come back six times. After that, you own it.

When I lecture, I ask questions to keep everyone engaged—to activate the secretary in each participant's brain. If I ask a question and someone answers it, all the other people stop thinking; their secretaries return to their desks without pulling the file. So when I ask questions during a lecture, I have to ask everyone to remain silent. It's the thinking process—the file pulling—that makes them strong.

After my success in Fargo, I was able to line up about six to eight conference gigs a year. It was an amazing time for me, each conference bringing me increasing accolades and a kind of celebrity status. When I would arrive at a conference, I'd be approached by people who had seen me speak before and wanted to thank me. People wanted to take pictures with me, and some even wanted my autograph.

But while I was reaching new professional highs,

something happened that would plunge me into a personal dark hole. President George W. Bush wanted to send troops to Iraq, and when Congress authorized him to use military force in October 2002, I believed I needed to be part of it.

I wanted to be with the troops. The pull is difficult to explain, and even now I have a hard time explaining it. My professional life was the best it had ever been; I was even becoming a kind of celebrity. I had a wife and family. *But I need to be there.* I'd been part of Desert Storm in Round One, and it ate away at me that I wasn't part of the effort to finish the job—especially now that I had both combat experience and medical training. I knew I could be an asset on the frontlines. I wanted to be back. I wanted a gun in my hand and an enemy to fight; I wanted a purpose, a channel, a reason for being. In my heart, I was a Marine.

I talked to recruiters. I even took a physical. For weeks, maybe months, Michelle and I talked it over. She would never have told me outright not to go. That wasn't her style. But every time I brought up rejoining the service, I could tell from her strained, anxious responses exactly how she felt about it. I was a father who ought to be there for his family.

It was around this same time that Michelle's brother, Tom, was diagnosed with non-Hodgkin's lymphoma. We were hopeful that he would respond well to treatment, but Michelle was of course stricken by the news and worried, although she didn't open up about it much. Here was another reason for me to be home with my family.

So I stayed. Not being able to be with the troops created a deep pit inside me. I became heavy, numb—the technical term is anhedonic, "without joy." I couldn't watch the news if it was about the war; it made me feel sick and stirred up, like I needed to vomit or punch someone. Before the war, I'd felt on top of the world in my work and teaching. Now I went through the motions, standing outside of myself.

I remember going to a 2002 Christmas party with Michelle and being unable to get out of the car. I couldn't talk to all those people pretending that everything was great, that anything mattered. I felt an emotional burden I couldn't explain.

When I trained in the martial arts, I trained just like I trained early on, with the intensity of seeing my brother get shot, thinking that if only I could have attacked the guy before he shot Billy ... Only now, as I pounded the bag, I'd be thinking *I am on the airplane that crashed into the World Trade Center. That guy has got a razor blade, and I've only got a microsecond to eliminate this threat.* Only in those hours with the bag did I feel alive, filled with purpose.

I knew in my head that I had a wonderful, rich, full existence and almost everything I'd ever wanted. But something was missing: my presence, my joy. I have never been medicated for psychological issues, but maybe I should have been then.

Alcohol wasn't what I needed, but during those dark days it was the medicine I chose. When my mind was racing and I had to relax, I drank. When sadness, confusion, resentment, or boredom swelled within me,

I drank. Booze was no longer a social lubricant; it was an increasing necessity just to make it through the sadness and anger that were my constant companions.

Months later, my depression about not being in Iraq finally began to fade. I wish I could explain why. It certainly wasn't my drinking. If anything, drinking prolonged it. Mostly I guess it just ran its course as I continued living each day and meeting my obligations. Besides, it was pretty clear the military did just fine without me.

As I pulled out of my depression, I started drinking less. I started to feel like my old self again—the John Bielinski who could juggle a PA job, a teaching job, lecturing gigs, a family, and physical training. I was back in charge.

But the imprint had been made. Alcohol was now my salve for the emptiness, a means of distracting myself from frustration, boredom, and pain. During those months, I had waded into the water, and it was only a matter of time before I would find myself in over my head.

For now, though, I was back to business as usual. I felt almost unbeatable. I was acing things clinically at the hospital, and I was a rock-star instructor.

I used my influence with students to set up a bike racing team to enter the annual Ride for Roswell, a fundraising event for the Roswell Park Cancer Institute in Buffalo. We raised $16,000 the first year, a figure that would explode to $46,000 the next. I said I was doing this in solidarity with my brother-in-law, who was still fighting cancer.

When I look back now, I roll my eyes. True, the

money was real and went toward an outstanding cause. But I didn't do it for Michelle's brother. I didn't do it for Michelle. I did it to feed my own ego—to be the star of the show. It's a weird sort of polarity—that money had nothing to do with me, and went to a really good cause; but in other ways, it was all about me. I really did help— and I helped for the wrong reasons. I don't know what to do with a contradiction like that. I do like myself better now that I admit my real motives, I'll say that.

One Saturday evening, Michelle and I were lying back on the couch watching some old black-and-white movie while Matthew played on the floor in his room. An ad came on, and I turned the volume down.

"Hey," she said. And just from the tone of her voice, I could tell it was important.

"Hey yourself," I said.

She laughed. "So I've been thinking." She wriggled around until she was sitting up, facing me. Her hair fell around her face in a way she would have thought was messy, but I thought was pretty as hell. "So I've been thinking. Matthew's almost two."

"Yep." I wasn't quite sure where this was going.

"And if we're going to have another kid—it doesn't really make sense to wait, does it?" She looked at me, half defiant, half nervous. "I mean if they're going to be able to play together. And I'm not getting any younger either, and—"

My stomach sinking, I interrupted her. "I want another baby, too." When her face lit up, I added quickly, "But there's one thing. It's a lot, taking care of a baby, right? It's a lot."

As if on cue, Matthew shouted, "MAMA! SEE!" from the other room. She smiled wryly.

"And I've got a lot going on now," I continued, "working, teaching that class, lecturing—which means traveling, too. I don't know if I can handle any more responsibility on top of all of that. I'd be letting you down all the time, you and the baby and Matthew."

Michelle turned her face away. In the long, sad pause that followed came the faint sound of Matthew's cheerful humming. *He must be building with his blocks*, I thought. That's when he hums.

"Or I could go part time," Michelle said softly.

I almost wasn't sure I'd heard her. "What?"

"Part time. If I went part time, I could take over more of the child care." Her face was flushed now—she rarely cried, but she had so much feeling in her eyes. "I'd do that. I'd totally do that. And we could afford it—"

"—we can afford it," I admitted.

We looked at each other in surprise. "So are we going to do it?" she asked.

We were.

What I'd said to Michelle was true: I was busier than I'd ever been. And when I told Michelle I couldn't handle more responsibility, I meant it.

And yet I managed to find the time for what *I* wanted.

A buddy and I were in a sports bar shooting the breeze, talking about the Sabres' chances in that night's game with the Canadiens. The bartender, a pear-shaped woman with a friendly, cherubic face, cut lemons and wiped at the bar with a dirty rag.

"Hey," my buddy said to the bartender. "You think

you can run and get us a couple more beers?"

She put down the rag she was wiping the counter with, rolled her eyes good-naturedly, and said, "Uh, I ran the Buffalo Marathon, so yeah, I think I can handle running you a couple beers."

I stared at her, my eyes running the length of her short, plump body. *What? A marathon? Her?*

As if reading my thoughts, she added, "Twenty-six point two miles, under six hours." She wiped her hands on her apron and poured our beer.

Once she was out of earshot, I said, "If she can do a marathon, we can *definitely* run one."

Does that make me sound like a jerk? Not gonna argue: I could be a total jerk back then, especially when my ego got involved. I decided I was going to run a marathon.

I quickly became obsessive about training, putting in long training runs at every opportunity. Michelle was pregnant, preparing for the new baby with hardly any help from me. As her stomach grew, the weight fell off me, my body shrinking and tightening from my training.

I purchased new running shoes right before the marathon—a huge rookie mistake. I started regretting them halfway through the race, feeling blisters being scraped into place on my feet. I actually stopped to buy bandages at a drug store, but even after I doctored up my feet, I was going slower than usual. It was going to be a tight finish.

The marathon organizers shut the race down after six hours, and anyone who doesn't finish within that time gets a DNF—Did Not Finish. The miles that I seemed to lope through during training runs were now a slog. Fifteen, sixteen, seventeen miles—*Damn, still nine more to go.* By mile twenty-one, I thought my thighs would break in two, each step bringing fresh misery.

Finally, I was within half a mile of the finish with just ten minutes to go. There was no way I was going to get a DNF, not after enduring all this pain. It would be as if I hadn't done it at all. I gutted it out, walk-running to the finish line with just seconds remaining. If you look up the 2003 Buffalo Marathon results, you'll see me: the five hundred and twentieth, and final, finisher, with a time of five hours, fifty-nine minutes, and forty-eight seconds.

Just ten days later—June 4, 2003—Michelle gave birth to our daughter, Sarah. I wish I could tell you about my fond memories of the day, but the truth is I can't form a firm recollection—I was just so full of my own shit, wrapped up in everything I was doing. If I'd given birth, I'd probably be able to tell you about every painful contraction and the euphoria of holding Sarah in my arms for the first time. But by this point, I was—distracted. I was looking and feeling phenomenal, down to my fighting weight. I was a star PA, an adored teacher, a celebrity lecturer, a marathon runner, and a family man. On the surface, things were wonderful, perfect.

I didn't realize that my life had become like the Las Vegas I'd recognized on my trip with my father. Underneath the glitz, pain and dishonesty were lurking. Behind the façade was the strange emptiness. I didn't know the cause then—all I knew was that the emptiness had to be filled. I felt I needed to fill it with accomplishments, to prove something, to be in control.

So after the first marathon, I wanted another. I continued my physical training, intent on improving on my marathon time. In 2004, I completed two marathons.

But it wasn't enough. Nothing was going to slow me down. I decided that marathons weren't enough; I wanted to try triathlons. So on top of everything else—work, teaching, lecturing, drinking, and being a father when I felt like making the effort—I now spent fifteen to twenty hours a week training for a half Ironman—a 1.2-mile swim, a 56-mile bike ride, and a 13.1-mile run. It was like I couldn't do enough, couldn't fill the void.

And what was Michelle doing during those extra fifteen to twenty hours a week that I was gone? Caring for a baby and a toddler, cooking meals, cleaning the house, picking up all the slack I was dropping. Watching TV by herself. Waking up alone, with me up before dawn to train. But of course, I wasn't thinking of all that then.

I wanted to push even further, train even harder. I set my sights on the biggest challenge I could think of, signing up for the 2005 Lake Placid Ironman triathlon: a 2.4-mile swim, a 112-mile bike ride, and a 26.2-mile run at the end. I started training harder than ever, spending almost all my free time squeezing in sessions. I had the discipline of a Marine, getting in the pool even when I was completely exhausted, forcing myself to get on the bike or hit the road even when the winter wind cut at my face.

That Christmas, in December of 2004, we went to Maryland to be with Michelle's family, rather than staying in Buffalo as usual. It was clear to me—to everyone, I think—that Tom was not going to get better.

But nobody talked about this; everyone kept the smiles glued to their faces, preferring not to acknowledge what all of us were thinking, that it was Tom's last Christmas.

I hated that, and it worried me. I tried to talk about it privately with Michelle, telling her that the family had to be prepared for the worst and try to support Tom and each other. She listened, but she seemed to put up walls around herself that I didn't know how to get through.

At the time, this surprised and frustrated me. In retrospect, it's hard to blame her. Between my work and teaching and physical training, my life had become all about me, me, me. Michelle and I used to talk effortlessly for hours. Now I was hardly ever around to talk with; I'd left her alone. It's no surprise that Michelle built emotional walls as a defense. The same walls that kept me from reaching her about Tom were what protected her from the hurt of my abandonment of our family.

All that spring, I kept it up: working, teaching, lecturing, training. Then, in April, Tom passed away, leaving the family shattered. There was so much anger, hurt, and confusion—in part, I believed, because no one had been prepared. They hadn't been able to have the necessary conversations. And now Michelle only retreated further—it seemed as though to stop herself from breaking, she grew hard.

I didn't know how to help her or fix the situation, and I didn't know how to stop. I guess Michelle didn't either. We desperately needed at least an honest conversation. Instead, we continued as a family, celebrating each other's birthdays and looking to the outside world like we had it all figured out.

But like a shark, I had to keep moving. I kept on working, teaching, lecturing, running, biking, swimming—doing my own thing. In July 2005, I completed the Lake Placid Ironman.

It took me sixteen hours. It began with the starter cannon at dawn. I waited for the first mass of people to get a few yards ahead before I started swimming in this mass start. Even so, soon people swam under me, over me—it was a tangle of flesh and bone. Threads of steam rose up around us as we muscled through the cold waters, the cheers of friends and families behind the gate on shore growing faint. Halfway through the swim, I saw a man draped over one of the buoys that lined the course, exhausted.

Once I staggered out, someone helped me rip off my wetsuit, and I ran barefoot toward my bike and gear. All around me people were strapping on helmets, slipping into bike shoes and neon shirts. And then we were off, up a steep tree-lined hill. People of all ages, and not all in typical "athlete" shape, pumped up that hill. The road ran along a creek, with a gorgeous view of the mountains, but after forty miles my quads were screaming so badly I no longer noticed—and I had seventy-two more miles to go.

Finally, as we approached town, people were lining the streets again, cheering us on. I'd made it. Once I'd jogged my bike over to its spot, it was time for the last portion: when we'd already given everything, we faced a full 26.2-mile marathon. Time to put my head down and just do it.

It was a feat of the human body more extreme than any I had ever attempted. Exhaustion swept through me in waves, but every time I found more strength. At one point we passed a red barn with a couple of horses grazing nearby. They glanced up at us in mild surprise: *what are you doing, ridiculous humans?*

I pushed on. I had trained and prepared for this race, and I was going to conquer it.

After sixteen hours of swimming, biking, and running, I approached the high school track where I would finish. I saw other athletes entering the track, running around it, and crossing the finish line on the straightaway. People formed a tunnel around me and the other competitors, cheering wildly. There were twenty thousand spectators urging us on.

Just as I set foot on the track, I caught sight of my family: Michelle, smiling tiredly after a long day, holding Sarah, with Matthew and Johnny at her side. I reached out and took Sarah from her, putting her on top of my shoulders. "Boys, run with me!" I shouted. Johnny and Matthew hurried and ran along with me, side by side, around the track and over the finish line.

I had done it. I kept setting bigger and bigger goals for myself, and I kept meeting them. I kept striving, working harder and harder to prove my worth to others and myself. I was like Icarus, flying higher and higher, closer and closer to the sun. I wanted to see how high I could go, how close I could get.

I didn't know that the wax holding my wings together had already started to melt.

Chapter 10

Storm Clouds

My first Ironman had filled me with a sense of purpose:
I was training to be a badass, to do something few
people could even contemplate doing. Finishing
the race had etched my name in the record book,
commemorating my accomplishment. It didn't make
a difference if someone was a thoracic surgeon or a
hospital CEO—I could always ask, "Did you ever do an
Ironman?" When the person shook their head, I'd think:
Didn't think so.

If you'd taken a snapshot of my life after that race,
you'd have thought I had it made. I'd completed one
of the greatest demonstrations of athleticism and grit
in the world. I was toned, athletic—at my peak. For all
our growing distance, Michelle remained a wonderful
wife, smart and dryly funny, a fantastic mother to our
healthy children. We even had a great dog, Dutchess, a

golden retriever who tumbled with the kids, ran with me, and curled up with Michelle at the end of the day.

The rest of my life looked just as good. Everyone fussed over me and made a big deal of me finishing the Ironman. I had spearheaded a wildly successful cancer research fundraising effort. I was respected at the hospital, developing a reputation for clinical excellence. Now teaching at two different PA schools, I was *the man* at both; if students were debating something another instructor had said, they came to me to help them. Some of my students started using the acronym WWJD to ask not what Jesus would do in a given situation, but what *John* would do. My ego was constantly being stroked and fed.

I loved it. I bought into it. If someone asked me how things were going, I would rattle off a list of my merit badge accomplishments. *I'm an Ironman, a kickboxer, a Krav Maga instructor, a combat Marine, a rock-star PA, a beloved instructor at two schools, a popular national instructor.*

And trust me, no one would have to ask me how things were going: I would remind them. I spent a lot of time flaunting my achievements.

Michelle knew me—she knew how I was always striving to be better, to be the best, to push the boundaries of achievement. "What's next," she joked after the race, "an Ironman on the moon?"

Funny she should ask. You might be surprised to learn that Buzz Aldrin, the second man to walk on the moon, battled depression and alcoholism after returning to Earth. He had done something amazing, making history, but once he'd accomplished this feat, he had difficulty readjusting to regular life. I hadn't walked on the moon, but looking back, I see that on some level I felt this same uneasiness. At the time, I thought I was running toward finish lines. Looking back, I was probably running from myself.

Where had all this striving gotten me?

I was trying to control everything in my life, figuring that if everything turned out the way I wanted, I would be happy and fulfilled. My career, my marriage, my family, my body, my hobbies: I was checking every single box, and yet in the months after the Ironman, all my satisfaction drained away, leaving emptiness. *Why am I doing all this?* I couldn't remember anymore. Was I living for myself? Was I living for my kids? Was I living for the grind? I didn't know. I was back on the ground, back on Earth, and I felt lost.

But at the time, I didn't have the tools to understand any of this. Feeling lost? Then keep on moving, John! Set more goals for yourself! Never let yourself think you're not in total control.

Work was an easy way to feel important and in control. I had six weeks of vacation per year at my hospitalist job, and I figured I could use that time to do a bit of freelancing as a PA. I landed a part-time gig in Arizona as a physician assistant three or four times a year. I would take a week's vacation from my full-time job and work an arduous stretch of twelve-hour shifts in Arizona. At week's end, I'd walk away with a check for $10,000 to $12,000.

The money wasn't the only thing I liked—the Arizona job was also an ego boost. The people at the hospital liked me because I was clinically sound and kept the line moving. They hadn't seen a PA like me—I functioned almost like an ER doc. They thought I was great, and they loved it when I was there.

I also enjoyed the freedom there. I didn't have to skirmish with Michelle about going out after work. When I wasn't on duty, I could spend my time gambling and drinking at nearby Laughlin casinos without having to worry about getting calls from Michelle asking where I was.

This arrangement seemed to work out just fine for Michelle, too. After her brother's death, Michelle had closed herself off—and while I tried to draw her out and comfort her, I didn't try as hard as I could have. Plus, I just wasn't around very much. And I was incredibly selfish. If I wanted to spend the weekend in Vegas with friends, that was as it should be. But God forbid Michelle would want to enjoy a girls' night out. I'd get pouty, passive-aggressive, resentful. I remember one Saturday when Michelle asked me to watch the kids while she went out for a couple of hours. I sulked, resentful at the loss of my freedom; I'd wanted to go to the bar to unwind from a long workweek. Not long after she'd driven off, one of the kids started crying. Eventually I got so mad, I kicked a door, meaning to knock it off its hinges. Instead, I broke my big toe.

Sometimes it almost seemed like we were in competition, like one of us had to lose for the other to win.

So Michelle seemed almost relieved when I would pack my bags for Arizona. She wouldn't have to worry about accommodating me. We may have lived in the same house, but increasingly we were more like roommates than a couple.

And that was fine with me—I was getting my ego fed elsewhere in my life.

I kept working, kept teaching, kept hustling. But still I found myself searching to fill that gnawing hole that was only getting larger after I finished the Ironman.

One day, a patient at the hospital said to me, "You know, I think you should consider becoming a Mason." He told me about the rich history of the Freemasons, the world's oldest and largest fraternity. To be a Mason would be to follow in the footsteps of George Washington, Benjamin Franklin, Winston Churchill, Davy Crockett, and even Harry Houdini. In order to join, he said, you had to be a man of good character with a belief in some supreme being.

Maybe this was it—what I had been searching for, something to give my life more meaning. So I went through the first stage of initiation, even hosting some lodge members at my house for the interview process.

But after learning more about the Masons' traditional altruism, I found myself drawing back. These were really *good men*—charitable and humble. Deep down, I knew my character wasn't sound. I may not have understood what exactly I was living for, but on some level I knew I wasn't Mason material. I was all about me. *This isn't just a merit badge. It's a fraternity of truly honorable men. And that's not who I am.*

Why didn't I decide *but that's who I could be*? Why did I draw back from this chance to be mentored into a better version of myself? I'm not sure, but I can guess: it wouldn't have fed my ego.

So I told the Masons I had decided not to pursue membership. Instead, I decided to train for another Ironman. After hearing me brag incessantly, Billy had decided he was going to try to complete his own Ironman, and I agreed to compete with him. I thought it would be a cool thing, two brothers doing the Ironman together—but the fact is, this second Ironman just wasn't that important to me.

Training for my first Ironman, I'd had discipline. I was out to prove something. This time, I just didn't have the fire. I kept on drinking, and my diet was shit: if I wanted chicken wings, I ate chicken wings. I remember one morning getting to the track for a ten-mile run. But before even getting out of the car, I realized I just didn't feel like it. I bagged the run. *One run isn't going to make that much difference*, I reasoned.

The problem was, these skipped sessions started adding up. I trained in a half-assed way.

On race day for the 2007 Lake Placid Ironman, Billy seemed nervous, but I was confident he'd do well. He had trained like a champion. It was myself I was nervous for; I knew I'd trained poorly. My mind raced: first up was a 2.4-mile swim, and I'd really neglected swimming in my training regimen. Lost in my thoughts, I was startled when a guy approached me and said, "Hey, did you do the Harriman half triathlon two years ago?"

"I did, yeah," I said, trying to figure out who he was.

"You yelled at me not to quit," he said with a smile.

"I didn't—I finished the race that day because of you. I'm here because of you."

All at once I remembered him. He had looked so weary and broken, trudging up a hill and breaking into a walk. "You'll hate yourself if you quit," I had shouted. "You can do this." I remember passing him and being sure that he was done, that he couldn't go on. I was glad to hear that his hard work had paid off, that his motivation had been strong enough, and that my encouragement had made a difference.

The cannon sounded with a deep boom, signaling the start of the swim. Instead of calmly waiting for the crowd to thin, like I had in my first Ironman, I swam with Billy into the churning mass of competitors. I was quickly overcome with feelings of anxiety and claustrophobia. Picture salmon trying to spawn in a crowded creek, and you'll have a good sense of what the beginning of an Ironman can be. Within ten minutes, I was panicked and exhausted, my heartbeat pounding in my ears.

John, calm down. Calm down. The more I told myself to relax, though, the more unsteady I felt. Somehow I gutted through the swim—wobbly, exhausted, and doubtful I was up to the 112-mile bike ride that came next.

Billy stayed with me as we started the first of two fifty-six-mile loops on the bike. It's illegal to draft in an Ironman, but Billy rode slightly in front of me to cut the wind, making my ride easier. No one was going to raise a fuss about a couple of non-elite competitors. My vision became fuzzy, and I felt weaker and weaker. I was probably dehydrated, and I'm certain my sodium level was low. I really thought I was going to crash; at one point, my eyes closed and I drifted—like I was falling asleep—before the road snapped back into focus. I wasn't safe.

"Billy, you've just got to go," I gasped. "I'm holding you back."

"No," he said. "C'mon, John. You got this, and I'm staying with you."

"We're almost to the end of the loop," I said. "I'll pull off there. I'll be fine. Kick some ass for me." I couldn't continue.

He turned and gave me a quick, worried glance before nodding and taking off. My sense of distance and time had been warped—I wasn't almost done with the loop, I had twenty-six miles to go. It took sheer will to keep pumping my legs, my thighs and lungs burning.

When I pulled off the course, I leaned against a brick wall and slid to the ground. I put my head in my hands and sobbed. I don't know how long I'd been there when Michelle showed up with the kids.

I wiped my cheek angrily, embarrassed, but Michelle just put a comforting hand on my shoulder. I looked up at her, and she looked at me sympathetically, keeping a reassuring grip on my shoulder. It was the first time I had felt support from her in a very long time.

When I look back on that day, I'm grateful for that memory of Michelle comforting me. She was giving me exactly what I needed—not ego-stroking or flattering attention, but love and understanding even when I failed.

Michelle helped me to the medical tent. Once I got some Gatorade in me I felt better, and we spent the rest of the day together. Billy did great, as I knew he would. He was always a great athlete.

Maybe things could have gotten better between me and Michelle after that. But I remained relentlessly selfish. Before, my selfishness swirled around my ego and how great I was. In the months that followed, I was consumed by my failure, my inability to finish my second Ironman. DNF. There was no way to rationalize a DNF. *Did Not Finish. Failed, couldn't do it.* Where my ego had been most swollen, now I was filled with doubt. *Maybe I'm not all that.*

Really, though, my doubts and fears were deeper than this single failure. I had understood mortality since I was just a teenager, and someone in my profession knows better than most people that life is fleeting. But for a long time—maybe ever since Billy got shot—I had been trying to exert total control over my life. Every time I was afraid or sad, this was my reaction, to gain control. Fighting, training, raising money for charity, making more and more money, gaining more and more praise and adulation. The Ironman was just the mirror that forced me to see the truth—my true powerlessness, my utter lack of control.

The emptiness inside me grew darker and deeper. Once again, I filled it with alcohol.

Drinking was now how I blew off steam and spent time with friends. I became a regular at a bar called Chester's, and I often hung out there with a fellow PA from my school, an older guy named Doug. Doug drank like I did, so we became fast buddies. He liked to throw money around, making us feel like we were big shots.

It was nothing for us to go into Chester's for lunch and drink until mid-afternoon, when I'd suddenly realize I had to get home to take care of my son. Sometimes I'd make it to the bus stop to meet Matthew; other days, he'd be standing at the front door, waiting for me to let him inside.

Doug already had two DWIs, but I figured he was smart enough to avoid getting another. But one night, Doug's girlfriend called me to ask if I knew where he was. I didn't, but I tried calling him repeatedly. I started getting concerned. It turned out he'd been arrested for a third DWI. He was also in trouble for writing bad prescriptions to strippers who wanted to get their hands on opiates.

In my mind, I was totally different than Doug. He had a problem, that was clear, but I didn't—*I was in control*, I kept telling myself.

I also became friends with the Chester's bartender, a guy named Kim. He was always friendly to me—and why wouldn't he be? I often racked up triple-digit bar tabs. Kim was a big drinker, and he did drugs, too. One Friday night, he was involved in a police chase. When I saw him at the bar the following Tuesday, he looked like he'd been through the wringer.

"How are you holding up, buddy?" I asked.

Kim looked me straight in the eyes and said, "John, I'm done. I'm done with it all." He said it with the sincerity of a dying man.

I didn't believe him. People didn't just *stop*. Even people with real problems, like Doug and Kim—let alone me. I still thought I was doing fine.

The more I drank, the less tolerance I had for anything that disrupted my equilibrium. That included crying kids, which made me shorter-tempered when Michelle left me home alone with Matthew and Sarah, who was now a toddler. I also started having blackouts.

I would stop for drinks after work and wake up the next day, not knowing how I'd gotten home. Even though I'd trained poorly for my second Ironman, I was still thin, so I decided that had affected my tolerance. I didn't think too hard about how I was stashing beer bottles in the couch, not wanting Michelle to know I'd drunk an entire twelve-pack. I didn't think too hard about the blackouts.

I didn't think too hard about any of it.

I still don't believe that my drinking affected me on the job, although there were some days when I'd spend a good amount of time hungover and hugging porcelain. One day I noticed the head nurse seemed to be in my face, much closer than would be considered normal or polite. I mentioned it to another nurse.

"You reek, John," she said. "You smell like a barroom floor. Chew some gum."

My drinking didn't slow me down on the lecture circuit. In fact, I looked forward to my lecture trips and the sense of celebrity they gave me. Lecture tours were hotbeds for partying—when I went out, there were always people eager to buy me drinks.

One night driving home from the bar, I lost consciousness and smashed into a stop sign. The impact jolted me awake, and somehow I made it home despite a badly mangled fender.

The next day, when Michelle asked about it, I told her I'd been the victim of a hit-and-run at work. I quickly replaced the car with a brand-new one.

When we'd had the new car for just a few days, I heard a telltale crunch and scrape from the driveway and ran outside. Michelle was bent over, inspecting the right rear fender of the new car, Matthew and Sarah by her side.

"What the hell?" I said angrily.

"Oh, I was backing out," she said, "and I nicked the fender of your new car—I'm so sorry. It's not too bad, though. I think we can—"

I exploded. "God *damn* it," I shouted. "Haven't even had it a *week*." I pulled my keys from my pocket and threw them as hard as I could, aiming for the windshield of Michelle's car.

Instead, the keys hit Sarah square in the face.

My heart froze. For a single, endless second, Sarah stood, mouth open in shock. Then she screamed in pain, hand flying to the red spot developing on one cheek.

Michelle picked up the wailing Sarah and rushed past me into the house; Matthew ran along after her, his face twisted in fear and confusion. He didn't look at me.

"Hey, listen," I said weakly. "I didn't mean ..." I trailed off.

At the door, pushing the kids inside, Michelle turned to me. "Who are you?" she whispered fiercely.

God, she's right. Who am I?

While things were fraying in my personal life, my PA work, which had always been a source of strength for me and my ego, started wearing on me as I treated more and more patients beyond helping. I'll never forget a case from the spring of 2008 when an ambulance brought me a sixteen-year-old boy who'd been hit by a train. People aren't usually transported to the ER after being hit by trains, because they don't usually survive. But this kid they transported.

There was absolutely nothing I could do for him. In one sense, I could accept this. Death comes with the job. But that wouldn't make breaking the news to the boy's mother any easier. As I waited for her, the boy's friends started showing up—wailing, screaming, crying. My thoughts turned to Johnny, who was just a year younger. I was a wreck. *Today it's this kid. Tomorrow it could be mine.* No one had told the boy's mother he was dead, so it fell to me. I was emotionally trashed for days afterward.

That weekend, Johnny had a hockey tournament, and Michelle said I still had to take him. Distraught, wild with grief over the boy's death, I took Johnny to the tournament. I drank the whole time, retreating into myself, not talking.

Around that time, I started having intense dark thoughts. I would come home exhausted from a long shift, ready to fall asleep. But as soon as my head hit the pillow, I'd start worrying about my kids. *They're going to die. And no matter what I do, I can't stop that.* As tired as I was, I'd stay wide-awake. I had to drink to be able to get to sleep.

Eventually I got a prescription for Ambien, but that made things worse. I still slept like shit, and when I got up in the morning, I would see sent text messages on my phone and emails in my outbox that I had no memory of writing—suggestive, flirty texts, loaded with typos. Not overtly toxic, but loaded with innuendo. Anyone who saw them would have known: this guy is bombed out of his mind.

Although the morbid thoughts mostly came to me at night, they could strike at any time.

One day, I took Sarah and Matthew to the Niagara River Recreation Trail. As the kids bounded along the trail, Dutchess weaving between them, I felt relaxed. Today was a picture-perfect postcard, cornflower blue skies above, tree-framed rock outcroppings, the churning waters flowing past us.

And then, out of nowhere, dark storm clouds gathered in my head. *What if one of my kids falls in the river? What if Matthew fell in? I'd jump in after him, but I wouldn't be able to save him. I'd be lucky to survive myself. Can I really protect them from anything? Bad thoughts? Bad influences? Illness, bad luck, death?*

"Hey guys, come here," I called out. "Give me a hug." I pulled them close, near to tears. "Let's go get ice cream."

I was beginning to understand what it would be like to be insane.

I was spiraling, but there was a part of me that was still planning and plotting, wanting to do more. I needed to do something to erase the shame of my DNF; I needed a new merit badge. I needed to regain control in my life somehow. I was still striving, holding the attitude that external validation would soothe the restlessness in my spirit.

I felt like I had topped out as a PA. I was at the

upper reaches of my earning potential, and there just wasn't any upside for me professionally. Yes, I could still save lives and help people get well. But I couldn't advance any further. But, I reasoned, if I earned my MBA, I could possibly look at becoming a hospital CEO. So in the fall of 2008, I enrolled in an executive MBA program at the University of Buffalo.

Yeah. It was crazy: a crazy, desperate, bound-to-fail idea. But my ego was flailing, drowning. I was desperate to feed it, to build it up again, make it nice and strong.

The courses were unbelievably difficult. The mathematics of accounting baffled me, and the accounting practices were well over my head. I think I actually got dumber sitting through class. I also couldn't fathom a business modeling course.

I couldn't fail. *I couldn't fail.* But it was so hard even to wrap my head around the concepts. I would sit down to study, knowing I really needed to do it, but my ego, terrified of impending failure, would race on. *Maybe if I go drinking or hit the casino, that'll relax me so I can study.*

With the semester drawing to an end, I was failing accounting and business modeling. When I had a make-or-break paper due in business modeling, I asked a classmate if I could take a look at his paper, telling myself it might "spur some ideas" for me. Instead, I did the unthinkable: I cheated. I took his work, moved things around a little, and submitted it as if I'd written the whole thing.

My classmate and I got an email from the professor. He noted the striking similarities in our papers and asked for an explanation. Even though I'd screwed this student by stealing his stuff, he covered for me. "John and I talked at great length about this issue as we prepared to write our papers," he explained. "Inevitably, we came to agreement on many points as we hashed out all the possibilities. But we wrote our papers independent of each other."

The professor dropped the matter. But now I was tormented by guilt. I was pursuing the degree to regain control, but everything I did was proving just how out of control I'd become.

Through the winter break, my conscience was in overdrive. *You cheated by stealing this guy's work and passing it off as your own, and then you let him cover for you? Some man you've turned out to be.* I felt shell-shocked, as though I was just sleepwalking through the days. There was only one thing I could do.

I emailed the MBA program director in early January 2009.

"I did something I'm very ashamed of. I cheated—I copied a classmate's paper and claimed it was my own. I just wanted to make you aware of what I did." Then I withdrew from the program.

Who had I become?

Chapter 11

Falling from Flight

Most of the time, I could rationalize just about any of my behavior—but not cheating. When I dropped out of the MBA program, it was for a simple reason: I'd been in over my head, and I had cheated.

When I told Michelle why I'd dropped out of the program, she shrugged. She knew how much I'd been struggling, and I honestly don't think she cared one way or the other. She may have retreated from me after her brother's death, but since then my increasingly selfish, impulsive behavior had been widening the distance between us. She'd learned that if I wanted to do something, there was nothing she could do or say to stop me. We lived at the same address but increasingly had our own lives. And we didn't argue well—we talked past each other instead of with each other, and we never confronted our problems. How could we? I was so wrapped up in myself and my increasing drinking that I couldn't see another point of view.

I was still stashing empty bottles under the couch cushions so Michelle wouldn't know how many I'd had, but there were more bottles than ever. I'd day drink, I'd drink after work. I never woke up with the shakes or the need to drink first thing in the morning, but it wasn't uncommon for me to get up to put the kids on the school bus and then sleep until noon because I was so hungover. My blackouts became increasingly frequent. Waking up not knowing how I had gotten home was becoming the norm. I'd part my curtains in the morning, see my car in the driveway and think, "How did I do this again?"

Of course, I never blamed the alcohol. I chalked my blackouts up to how I drank—*I've lost too much weight, I need to switch from hard liquor to beer,* or *It's the Ambien, it's changing my brain.* I knew I was drinking a lot, but I told myself I was managing it. I would switch to beer and feel like I was in control, and I wouldn't think too much about it when I went back to Jack and Cokes a few days later.

Some of my best drinking buddies were my students. A lot of them looked at me as the cool professor—not only a guy who worked in the field and lectured nationally, but the one who went by his first name and partied with them. I saw them as the cool kids, and boozing it up with them made me feel cool, too.

So I was surprised when—at the start of the spring 2009 semester—all the students who had been assigned to my hospital for rotations dropped off my schedule.

I went to see the scheduler, who, avoiding my eyes, said simply, "Those students opted not to come do a rotation with you."

What was going on? My site had always been the students' favorite.

Soon afterward, the program director asked me to come see her about a budgetary issue, but I quickly realized our conversation was about something else. She seemed almost afraid, reluctant to address the issue at hand, but eventually she got there: my drinking was making students uncomfortable. I was getting a reputation for using inappropriate language and giving preferential treatment to my drinking buddy students.

An image flashed through my mind: the pained, appalled face of a redheaded female student in a group I'd been hanging out with outside of class. I'd been drunk that night, straight from a meeting of the Hash House Harriers, a running club that was really more a drinking club. The Hash had a bawdy atmosphere, with everyone going by edgy nicknames—mine was "High Baller"—and constantly making innuendo-rich remarks. When I met up with my students, I was still in that frame of mind, as well as several drinks past where I should have stopped.

"I'd like to get a hotdog," the redheaded girl said cheerfully.

"I'll show you a foot-long," I fired back.

This comment would have been appropriate, appreciated, and in good taste at the Hash—but in front of students, it was not appropriate. I was always good at reading people, and her shocked face and the group's sudden silence told me I'd made a misstep. I hurried to bury what I'd said, trying to mitigate the damage, swerving. But that moment is part of a collage of uncomfortable moments, a patchwork quilt of things I've said and done that still make me cringe to remember. It's only now that I can look back and see the ego and the posturing. At the time, I wasn't present—the water was rising, but I'd convinced myself I liked the rain.

Now the program director looked at me steadily, working up her courage. "That kind of behavior threatens the integrity of our entire program."

"It will never happen again. Never. I promise you that."

And I meant it. I fully intended to get things under control.

But near the end of that semester, one night I couldn't sleep and popped an Ambien. When that didn't help, I had a few drinks. And when I woke up, I saw I'd spent the night texting with students—mostly harmless remarks, but others better suited for gatherings of the Hash.

My mind raced. I couldn't let the program director find out from someone else. I had to man up. I figured a direct approach would be best. I went to her office and made a full confession, even showing her the texts. "I just wanted to let you know what happened," I said.

She set a pen on a stack of papers, pulled off her reading glasses, and looked me in the face. "John, do you think you have a problem?" she asked. "Do you need to get some help?"

A problem? Help? Fuck you, I thought. I shook my head.

"If you're willing to get help ..." she said. She was

clearly distressed and uncertain of what she should do. I was a highly respected instructor for the program, having elevated the program's reputation substantially over the time I'd been there. But this was unacceptable, and I knew it.

And yet I just kept shaking my head. I didn't need *help*.

She furrowed her brow and picked up her reading glasses. "I need some time to figure out what to do with this."

As I left her office, I realized she was going to either order me to get help or fire me, neither of which sounded good. Being fired would hurt my ego. Having to "get help"—confront my drinking, confront my behavior, look at what lay beneath them both: that felt unendurable, unthinkable.

I resigned my position.

The semester had just ended, so I wasn't abandoning my students. I justified my departure to Michelle—and myself—saying that I was tired of the strict and oppressive classroom environment and wanted to focus on my creative lecturing.

Lecturing at conferences was the best. For one thing, I didn't just go and give one lecture. I routinely gave three or four per conference—feeding my needy ego, making me feel important. The people who went to the conferences also fed my needs. I'd be walking through the hotel lobby and I'd hear, "Oh my God! I saw your talk. It was awesome. Can I buy you a beer?" And then I'd have my drinks paid for the rest of the night.

The conferences were always in nice locations—maybe a Disney compound, someplace near the beach.

No driving was necessary. So yes, the conferences provided some of the best drinking times, a way to drink with impunity and with a lot of intention— intention to get carefully, exquisitely hammered. I was far away from Michelle's disapproving looks, so I didn't have to push away the feeling that she was right. Once I'd given my lecture, I had no responsibilities, so it didn't make any difference whether I came home at ten o'clock at night or two o'clock in the morning. I wasn't going to catch any crap about what time I came in.

There's a part of me that wishes I could go back and pull that version of me's head out of my ass. I wish I could have understood Michelle's disapproval as a wake-up call and act of love. But that's not the way life works.

Billy would sometimes come along with me to my conferences in Palm Springs, California, where we would drink and party together. Once I even involved him in my lecture, telling the audience that we had a real expert in the house. "If anybody has any questions at all, don't hesitate to ask Billy," I said seriously. At one point in the lecture I said, "Hey Billy, how bad is it when there's free air in the diaphragm?" His face grew somber as everybody craned their necks to hear his response. "Really, really bad," he said. We cracked each other up, being our usual immature selves. Once, in a crowded men's bathroom, I yelped at Billy, who was at the urinal next to mine, and shouted, "Hey buddy, quit looking at my penis!"

Billy gave it right back to me. "I can't help it," he responded dreamily. "It's like a lava lamp—I can't look away."

By 2010, I had lectured about emergency medicine to thousands of people. I had become an expert at engaging audiences and helping them internalize the lessons they would most need as medical professionals. I would start with a hook. "Who knows this song?" I'd ask, before launching into a rendition of Toby Keith's "Who's Your Daddy." Someone would guess right, and I'd make a joke about how great a singer I was. Then I would announce that when it came to chest pain, what people really had to remember were the five "can't-miss" causes of chest pain—and to do that, they should use the acronym PAPPA. "I want you to say it with me, folks. Who's your PAPPA?" They said it, laughing, and then said it again louder. When I talked about patients with pulmonary symptoms, I warned audience members not to make "a HORID mistake." I didn't know these acronyms were spelled wrong—and the beautiful thing was, it didn't matter. People would flood me after my lectures, to the point that I had to take questions outside. "I wish I could watch your lecture again," people told me.

The North Carolina Academy of Physician Assistants (NCAPA) approached me about filming my emergency medical conference and selling the videos. Under the deal, I'd get a third of the profits. I was ready to pull the trigger until the group's CEO asked me to give up the copyright to the material. That was a deal-killer to me. *Fuck that. I can do this by myself.*

Surprisingly, when I floated the idea to Michelle, she was all for it. We'd reached a point where if I said it was a nice day out, she'd say it was too windy. But she was enthusiastic about the idea of this business, and I was grateful for the support. So in early 2010, with $20,000 in savings, a $10,000 loan from Billy, and a $10,000 loan from my dad, I started my business as an LLC: Who's Your PAPPA Seminars. I had a feeling this could be huge.

For my first video, I got permission from Westfield Hospital to use the conference room on a Sunday. I asked a lab tech named Elaine to film me and edit the video, telling her she could keep the camera as payment. She set up the camera and trained it on me, just standing in front of a whiteboard. This was a much smaller crowd than I was used to—I made jokes to the camera and felt awkward when Elaine just stood there, her expression stern behind her glasses. We kept filming for hours, and although the footage wasn't exactly my best work, I figured it was better to have something done than nothing. This was just the beginning.

It was not uncommon for me at this time to work a twenty-four-hour shift at the hospital, be off for twelve hours, and then come back on for another twenty-four-hour shift. Because the hospital was more than an hour from home, I'd often sleep there—but not before drinking heavily after hours. I know there were times I reported for duty when I wasn't at my best self, hungover and queasy. To this day I don't believe my patient care was compromised, but I know I wasn't always the best I could be.

Of course that's what I *want* to believe; it's what I hope is true. But there's no question that as much as I was running myself down and dulling my senses with booze, I increased the chances of serious error.

I'd also been having more and more conflicts at the hospital. Once, irritated at the manager of the x-ray lab for writing up a nurse friend of mine, I wrote her a scathing letter. My letter wasn't intended to set the record straight; I wanted to hurt the manager. I taped the letter to her door before sleeping at the hospital. *I'm going to show her.* In the morning I had second thoughts and quickly ran down to her office to retrieve the letter, but I was too late. Her door was open.

With actions like that, I was pulling the weight of the establishment down on me. My clinical work was still top-notch, but I was emotionally unstable, causing lots of damage and hurting people. I wanted what I wanted *now* or there'd be hell to pay. People started distancing themselves from me; my world was shrinking by the day. My ego was so big, there wasn't room for anybody else. At no time did anyone at the hospital confront me about my drinking—not that it would have done any good. But it had to be common knowledge. And drinking or not, I'd become an emotional wrecking ball.

In the spring of 2010, I decided to leave my job at Westfield for Miller Suburban Hospital, which was closer to our house. I rationalized this to myself: I could run to work now instead of driving more than an hour each way. But deep down, I knew I was losing friends at Westfield, losing people's respect, losing their patience. I ran away.

I went into my new job thinking I was a real hotshot—a nationally recognized lecturer with his own business. The people at the hospital didn't want to hear any of it. To them, I was a commodity PA, and I needed to shut up and do my job.

Fine. I figured they'd learn soon enough. I was *good*.

That summer, I grew my business. I knew my lectures were excellent, but my videos had to be better. So I arranged to tape my next set of lectures, inviting all my friends and family to be in the audience, and I hired a professional videographer.

Every time I got a DVD order, I got an update on my phone that made the tiny sound of a cash register clanging shut. *Ching! Ching!* Business was growing fast. I explored Facebook and internet marketing and figured out new ways to sell my products. Orders started rolling in—but I started getting calls from angry wives. "What is this *Who's Your PAPPA* I'm seeing on my credit card statement?" they asked. So I changed the name of the LLC to sum up my views on medicine: CME4LIFE. CME is the commonly-used abbreviation for continuing medical education.

My business was providing me with inspiration and direction, yet I still knew something was wrong in my life. I had a sense of impending calamity, but I had no idea what it was. Although it sounds ridiculous now, it didn't occur to me that I had a drinking problem, though if I'd been listening to what Michelle was trying to say, it might have. *Maybe I need to be a more moral person*, I thought.

I had heard a lot about a megachurch called The Chapel, so I decided to visit—but with a giant chip on my shoulder. When I stepped into the vast, high-ceilinged room, airy and spacious despite the three thousand people in attendance, I thought: *This has to be a scam. Who's making all the money in this joint?* At one point in the service, the preacher asked people visiting for the first time to raise their hands. I raised mine, but I was resolute: I am not falling for any of your crap.

My church experience had been limited to the conservative and sedate Catholic Mass, and I didn't know what to make of this place where people swayed, sang, and raised their hands in the air. It was weird to me. But there were electric guitars in the band and I kind of liked the music, which I found catchier than traditional Catholic hymns. I started to feel a presence in the music—reluctantly, but I felt it nonetheless.

I wasn't ready to make a commitment, but I kept coming back because of the music. The music director was a guy named Benji, and every week he'd say a few words, sing some songs, and get everyone to sing along. I found a lot of the people to be kind of freaky, but the minister, Pastor Jerry, wasn't bad and the music was damn good.

But I also wasn't convinced that this was what I needed. This church was new—foreign—and I also needed to go back to something I knew. I needed to find my North Star. I returned to the Krav Maga fighting school, which I'd drifted away from as I'd become more absorbed in drinking.

I was surprised to see a familiar face: Benji's. He was stronger than me but untrained. We started sparring together, rougher and rougher, and became friends. When I decided to take some private classes at the Krav Maga school, I paid for Benji to get lessons, too, in exchange for guitar lessons from him. And I kept going to the church. It was comforting to me to know Benji was there. We would sometimes talk a little about spiritual matters, but only briefly. Sensing my uncertainties, Benji once told me, "You can't really have faith without having doubt. You can't have faith without questioning." He wasn't trying to convince me, but I knew he'd be there for me if I had any questions.

But despite the church, and despite the Krav Maga training, by late September 2010, I felt like a storm was brewing. Something calamitous was about to happen.

So I doubled down on what I knew: I kept drinking—and I kept fighting.

During one of my rotations in Arizona, I went out after work with colleagues to a tired, quiet bar. We weren't there long before I noticed a drunk guy by a pool table being generally obnoxious and a bully. I didn't like him, but I figured he could do his own thing.

As my group got into our drinking and socializing, I kept hearing this guy being a punk to some people near the pool table. So I decided I was going to shoot some pool—not necessarily to antagonize the guy more, but maybe send a message that he should move on.

"You stole my money!" he yelled. "What'd you do with my quarters?" He walked up on me and I knew he wanted a fight. Well, because of my Krav Maga training, I knew I could put this guy on his ass without throwing a punch. There's a divot just under the Adam's apple called the manubrial notch. Push some fingers in there and you can launch someone across the room. I wasn't about to let this guy get close enough to throw a punch. As soon as he got within range, I put two fingers into the notch and pushed, launching him twenty feet across the bar. That's when all hell broke loose. The police came—for him—and at first I felt vindicated, like I'd performed a public service by subduing this ass. *You're doing great*, I kept on telling myself. *You're in control.*

But the feeling of doom intensified. I was okay this time, but what if the guy had pulled a gun? Krav Maga wouldn't have saved me if he'd shot me from across the bar. I thought back to all my close scrapes through the years. I was a lucky bastard, but sooner or later my luck would run out. The sky was growing darker.

In October of 2010, Michelle said she was going to take the kids to visit her parents in Maryland. I felt the old familiar giddiness, that spring break feeling. *I'm going to party hearty.* I couldn't wait for them to get out the door.

Once they left, I hopped in the shower and then headed to a bar downtown where I could drink and let off steam. When I went to the bar to order, I was surprised to see Kim at the counter—my old bartender from Chester's.

"Kim!" I said. "Fancy meeting you here. Buy you a drink?"

"John," Kim said seriously, "I haven't had a drink or done drugs since the night I was chased by the cops. I've turned my life around."

"Come on," I said in disbelief.

"I'm serious," he said. "I started going to twelve-step meetings."

"Yeah?" I said dubiously. "And what does that do for you? How do you feel?"

"Peaceful," he said truthfully. "I don't have any of the same friends. Now I have friends who care about me and really, authentically, no-kidding care how I'm doing."

Against my will I thought of all the friends I'd lost. "Yeah?"

"Yeah. And sometimes, I know it sounds funny, I'll just go to the park and watch kids playing and feel so grateful and so at peace."

I felt a chill. I hadn't felt at peace in years—maybe ever. I was always on the move, collecting merit badges, thinking my accomplishments would make me happy. But the more I succeeded, the less peace I felt. The less peace I felt, the more I drank, and drank, and drank, creating pain and drama for those around me, losing friends, losing the respect of my coworkers, losing the respect and intimacy of my own wife.

And then it hit me.

Fuck me. I'm an alcoholic.

I went back to my seat and slumped into it, oblivious to the people around me. My life was out of control. I knew I was fucked, I knew I was falling.

And once I stopped to look, I could see it all, the collage of chaos I'd caused, the painful things I'd said and done. The deplorable way I ignored Michelle and the kids. My inappropriate behavior with students. Treating colleagues with disrespect. Getting into bar fights.

I got up from my chair and stood at the bar, waiting for Kim to get free so I could ask him a question. With a weird patience, like I was in a dream, I stood there listening to the orders shouted around me: *Double shot of Jameson! Jack straight up! Another pitcher here!*

When the crowd finally cleared, Kim walked up to me, wiping his hands on a grubby cloth. "Kim," I said. "How do you … how do you start?"

The next day, I went to a twelve-step meeting called the Eye Opener.

Any resolve I'd felt after talking to Kim quickly melted away as soon as I arrived. The meeting was held in the basement of an old, shitty church with loose linoleum tiles and a stale, musty odor. Once I found the room, I scanned it and saw a bunch of people I instantly despised. *Fuck you guys. I don't like you. I may have a problem, but I'm not a loser like you.* I was so angry to be in this place that I could feel my heart thumping in my chest.

When they asked if this was anyone's first meeting, I raised my hand. *Fuck you all.*

I remained mostly silent until near the end when the guy moderating the discussion asked me if I had anything to say.

"Yeah," I spat. "I'm an alcoholic—but I'm not ready to stop." I paused, my fists clenched on the table. "I'm an alcoholic but I'm not ready to quit drinking. I don't want to quit drinking."

After the meeting, the moderator approached me. "You should have brought that up earlier," he said. "We could have formed the meeting around the topic."

Well, fuck you, too. It was my first meeting.

He placed a coin in my hand representing twenty-four hours of sobriety, and he gave me a stack of sobriety literature.

I hid the papers at home, not wanting Michelle to see I'd been to a meeting while she was out of town.

But I stopped drinking. I kept on going to meetings. And—come on, were you expecting a miracle?—I didn't hesitate to let everyone else there know they were doing it wrong. Didn't they know I was a powerful lecturer and a successful business owner? They might need DWIs and broken families to stop drinking, but I didn't—I was managing things just fine.

Over the next few weeks of sobriety, I started feeling a little better physically, but it's not like my life was getting better. I still wasn't fitting in at my new job, so I gave them my notice, saying I would stay through the new year. Even without alcohol, I felt the same as always, acted the same as always.

Then I had to attend Billy's stag party in Vegas—he was marrying a girl he'd met at one of my conferences in Palm Springs. It was a Jack and Jill party, so Michelle came with me.

On our way to Vegas, Michelle asked me what she should do if I tried to drink. I had told her flatly, "You have nothing to do with it."

It was simple in my mind—I thought I had a choice and that I could make a conscious decision to not drink. I had not yet come to terms with the fact that I was an alcoholic, and that I had long ago lost the power to choose. I spent the first night sober, and was completely miserable.

The second night I decided to put an end to my misery.

There was nothing Michelle could say to stop me. "It's my choice," I remember saying. "I *could* stay sober tonight, but I am choosing not to."

Michelle just sighed and looked away.

The second night my misery was even worse. I couldn't drink enough to get that buzz, to find the magic from the alcohol. It was hell—I couldn't drink, but I couldn't *not* drink. I was completely powerless.

After returning from Vegas, by some miracle, I was again able to refrain from drinking for a little while longer. I was drinking a ton of coffee, so much my teeth were getting stained. I got my teeth whitened.

I hadn't expected it to *hurt* so much. I was miserable, and my teeth hurt like a motherfucker. I started telling myself that this was completely unreasonable.

The next afternoon, I called the dentist and said my teeth were killing me. "Go get drunk," she said. "You'll feel better in the morning."

I hung up and turned to Michelle. "The doctor ordered me to get drunk," I said, trying to sound lighthearted. She knew I was going to meetings and hadn't drunk in weeks. The dentist's order was a catalyst for me. It was the perfect excuse for me to slip back into my old ways.

Things got back to pre-twelve-step normal after that. My business was thriving, I was as busy as ever, and though I'd gone back to drinking, I told myself I had everything under control.

Just after Christmas 2010, lightning struck: I received notice that I was being audited after some possible irregularities in my Schedule C filing were flagged by the IRS. I had told my accountant he could be creative, but when I saw just how creative he'd gotten, I was floored. There was no way I could justify some of the write-offs he'd put down for my expenses.

Michelle was completely undone, immediately thinking we would be ruined. "It'll be okay," I kept telling her.

"I hate you for what you've done," she said to me at one point.

I didn't stop to think too hard about what she meant.

So instead, while the audit crawled slowly on in the background, I focused on opportunities. There was this bar trick I would do to people that completely convinced them I was psychic—every time I did this trick, people almost fell over in astonishment. I hatched a plan to get people's reactions on video to generate some web traffic for my business.

So on January 4, 2011, I got some of the few people from the hospital that I got along with to film me doing this trick on people at a bar. Over the course of the evening, I got pretty drunk—and pretty quickly. I remember calling Michelle at eleven o'clock.

"You coming home?" she asked.

I assured her we were almost done.

"You sure you're okay? You're slurring your words."

"Never better," I said crisply.

I just wanted to keep the party going. I had to work the next day, but it was my last day at Miller Suburban before starting my new job—I could be a little hungover, I figured.

When I finally left the bar in the early morning hours, I could barely stand up straight. When I tried to pull out of my parking spot, I backed into a car—with people in it. They got out quickly to inspect the damage.

I got out, too. "That's nothing," I said. "I'll pay for it."

I could see one passenger quickly dialing his cell phone—calling the police.

I got back in the car, put it in gear, and peeled out.

I struggled to stay in my lane—it took all my concentration. I thought I was doing great until I noticed the flashing lights in my rearview mirror.

Shit. Shit. Oh shit.

What I remember most is how the police officers treated me like a gentleman. As we stood at the side of the road in the freezing dark, slush slowly soaking into my shoes, trees swaying tall and black behind me, me trying not to sway, he said politely: "Sir, you're drunk and you're under arrest. Do you understand what we're saying?"

"Yes, sir." I responded. Suddenly my mind started to clear as the cops quietly escorted me to the back of the squad car.

The click of handcuffs is a very cold and distinct sound.

I was in real trouble. My life would never be the same.

At the police station, I stood at the cell door as it slid closed in front of me and asked the officer if I could shake his hand. "Thank you for treating me like a gentleman," I said, as I reached through the bars.

As I sobered up in the cold, ugly holding cell, my mind wouldn't stop racing. *I'm fucked. Everything is ruined. Michelle will probably leave me and take the kids. I'll lose my job. I won't have anything.*

Eventually an officer allowed me to make a call. Michelle picked up the phone and said, "Don't bother coming home." I was confused, desperate. I felt like I was in a nightmare.

"No, wait, you don't understand," I said. "I'm in jail."
To say those words to her—it was an earthquake inside me. I felt like I'd sailed straight into a storm—and I didn't know if I would ever make it back to shore.

On Michelle's end of the line, for a long time, there was only silence.

Chapter 12

Revelations

I stood at the counter as the officer handed me my belt and shoelaces. "Thank you," I said, my voice sounding hollow and strange. I was still, maybe, a little drunk. Michelle had said she would pick me up on her lunch break, but they were releasing me early.

I stepped outside into the frigid morning air, my breath forming puffs in front of me. The cold air was a tonic, easing the throbbing at my temples. Everything felt so disconnected, so surreal: here I was, emerging from the police station. Nothing would ever be the same again.

What was I supposed to do? The jail was on the same road as Michelle's office, but seven miles away. I decided to walk.

My mind was bedlam: confusion about how much trouble I was in, scared about the potential consequences with the law and with Michelle. For the first several miles of my walk, I trudged along, barely noticing my surroundings, my mind ricocheting from thought to thought. *My name's going to end up in the newspaper. My reputation will be shot. God, Michelle's going to kill me. Leave me? How do I tell my kids? Who have I become? I disgust myself.*

Halfway to Michelle's office, a sign caught my eye—it was a law office. I squinted at the name on the sign, trying to quiet my thoughts and figure out why it was familiar. In a flash, I remembered: I had met this lawyer when he brought his elderly mother into the ER a few weeks back. We'd hit it off. I had expedited their visit, saving them a couple of hours. "I owe you a favor," the man had said, handing me his business card. "If you ever need anything, call me." A tiny glimmer broke through my confusion and desperation. I would call the lawyer later—maybe he could give me some advice about my situation.

And then I kept on walking, miles and miles to go.

My life, as I had been living it, was unmanageable. I'd been out of control, and now I was a broken man. Was Michelle willing to help me and support me, or had I finally so destroyed her trust that she was ready to leave me?

When I got to her office I waited in the overheated lobby, sitting on a hard chair, staring at my feet. I figured I would just wait there until her lunch break. But the friendly young woman at the desk recognized me. "John! You're Michelle's husband, right? I'll let her know you're here."

When my wife came into the lobby, pulling her coat on, she had her work face on: impassive and cool. "Let's go," she said as I got to my feet.

In the car, though her face stayed impassive, Michelle gripped the steering wheel so hard her knuckles went white. Even seeing her anger in that moment—that was the least of it. I was absolutely numb, cold, and lost.

Still, I wanted to say something. But I didn't know what to say. Outside the car, slush sprayed under our wheels. Inside, the silence was deafening.

Finally, her jaw so tight I could barely understand her, Michelle said, "Is this your bottom?" Her eyes never moved from the road.

I knew instantly that a lot—maybe everything—was riding on how I answered. As the car ground relentlessly over the slush and asphalt, my exhausted ego groped for the right thing to say—something that would impress her, soothe her, show her I could regain control. I thought about pronouncing a grand pledge that from here on out, as God was my witness ...

Even before I said it, I could hear it for the lie it was. I stared out into the bright, harsh winter light. "I sure hope so," I said softly.

As weak as it was, as small as it was, it was one of the most honest things I'd ever said. Then, to my horror, a shudder rose in my chest. In seconds, I was sobbing, as quietly as I could, but sobbing, deep hiccupping sobs like a broken-hearted kid.

I pressed my aching forehead against the cold window. I couldn't imagine feeling lower than I felt at that moment.

Now, finally, Michelle looked at me. "Okay," she said. "It's going to be okay." She was torn, I could see—full of rage, but able to see that I was shattered. She didn't know what to do or where we were headed, either.

All I wanted to do was dissolve into sleep and wake up from this nightmare; but so many things had to be done. I called in sick to the hospital on what was supposed to have been my last day of work. Michelle went to pick up Matthew from school. He knew I was in jail—he must have heard Michelle on the phone with me the night before—and had been so upset in class that he couldn't function.

Once they got back, I sat Matthew down on the couch with me. My son, ten years old, looked at me with red-tinged eyes heavy with worry. I know I still looked like I'd been through the rinse cycle of a washing machine.

"It's because of the government, right?" he asked, his face crumpling.

That threw me. "What?" I asked, putting my arm around him.

"Because of the tax audit?" he asked, wiping his face.

My heart broke. We'd been so fucking stressed about the tax audit.

"I know you're scared because I was in jail," I told him. "It scared me, too. But this has nothing to do with the tax audit. Please don't worry about that."

I stopped short, choosing my words very carefully. I hated myself in that moment. *He idolizes you, and you try to teach him to be good, and you're a fucking hypocrite.*

"I know you're worried, and I owe you an explanation. Last night your dad did something bad." I took a breath.

"I drank a lot of beer and then I tried to drive home. And when I was driving, I hit another person's car, and I should have stopped, but I didn't. And then I kept driving, even though I'd had too much to drink, which is very dangerous. But the police stopped me before I could do any more damage."

Matthew stared at me. "Why did you do that?"

I said carefully. "I wasn't thinking clearly. But I'm going to get better. I'm going to work really hard."

He buried his face in my chest and I wrapped my arms around him. "I'm glad you're home," he said.

"I love you."

There was so much more to do, so much reckoning to be done, small and large. I had to fix myself. I had to get better. I couldn't *pretend* to be better. I had to *get* better. Stephen Covey says that you can't talk your way out of something you have behaved yourself into; you have to behave your way out of it. That's where I was. I'd run out of excuses. I'd run out of rationalizations. I had to fix myself and, to whatever extent I could, fix the mess I'd made.

The small reckonings were easier. I got my car, which had been impounded. I called the lawyer whose name I had recognized on the sign, reluctantly telling my story and asking if he knew any attorneys who could help me. "John," he said, "These are the cases I do. I represent DWI cases all the time, and I owe you a favor. Let me help you." When he asked which judge was going to preside over my trial, I told him, and he informed me he had worked on that judge's election campaign.

Maybe this was a coincidence—but I didn't believe it was. At the time, it felt to me like the first divine spark of encouragement on my long path of redemption.

Then I began the deeper reckonings. I found a twelve-step meeting. I walked in, my feet and heart heavy. It hadn't been so long ago that I'd been at another sobriety meeting, telling everyone that, unlike you fuckups, I've got everything under control. Yeah, right.

In this meeting, I didn't speak. I sat in that folding chair, on the dirty linoleum, next to a lot of people with their hearts open, and listened. I listened as a desperate man. I listened as a broken man. Before, I'd been too full of myself to listen like this. But now that my heart had cracked open as well, I saw my own sad heart in everyone who spoke. I saw how we were all the same; I saw myself in them, and them in me.

After the meeting, I approached one man I knew from previous meetings. He was a fellow Marine, and I suspected he despised me. Whenever I'd spoken in a meeting, he'd get up to get coffee, as if unable to tolerate my bullshit—at least, I guessed that now, and I didn't blame him.

I went up to him, tears in my eyes, and said, "I got a DWI last night."

He saw my desperation. He saw I needed help. And he was there. He sat down and talked to me without judgment, without any hint of resentment toward me for my past behavior. And when we were done, he gave me a twenty-four-hour sobriety coin—a kind of talisman to help me go another twenty-four hours—and his phone number, telling me to call him at any time I was tempted to drink or just needed to talk.

Twelve-step meetings were one reckoning I was just beginning to meet. In some ways, an even harder one was the reckoning with my wife. With her, I felt like I was walking on a frozen pond, unsure how thin the ice was. Was I about to fall through? Would frigid darkness close all around me? Michelle was teetering on the edge of leaving me, unsure if what we had was worth saving. I couldn't blame her. But God, I didn't want her to go.

She came with me to my third post-DWI twelve-step meeting, an angry, seething presence who literally radiated heat. Her shoulders were as hard and set as a Marine in battle. She sat beside me on the cold metal chair, erect and stiff, not speaking, not even looking at me.

When it was her time to share, she looked around at my fellow alcoholics. "Honestly, I don't know if John is an alcoholic or just an asshole," she said. "I don't know whether I can live with him anymore." She paused, all eyes upon her, every word a dagger. "And I don't know whether he's coming here to get better or whether it's just more bullshit to stay out of trouble."

My face burned as I realized that I didn't know either. *Is this all just an act, or is it real?*

It is a strange, disorienting place, this kind of knowing but not knowing. As an alcoholic—and I've heard others say the same—I had grown so used to lying to myself and others that it seemed like the only normal way to live. At some point, I realized I'd been lying for so long that I couldn't tell anymore what was lie and what was truth. Rationalization, lying, bullshit: these had become more than habit; they were fused to me, almost part of my DNA. I hated liars, and I had become the biggest one I knew.

So I was going to have to break myself down and rebuild—tear off the old façade without any certainty that my new self would survive. The ego takes any kind of spiritual growth as an insult; the ego rebels. And I had a hell of a powerful ego.

The very first of the twelve steps is to admit powerlessness over alcohol and acknowledge the unmanageability of one's life.

Maybe surprisingly, this one I was confident of. Even I could see it now: I had no power over myself when I drank, and no power to "choose" whether to drink. When I called Billy to let him know what had happened, I said, "I'm done. I'm done drinking."

"Aw, dude, you had a bad night."

"You don't understand: I'm done. I can't drink—ever again."

The second and third steps, however, were more difficult for me. Although I'd felt a peace and rightness at The Chapel that I'd never experienced within the Catholic church, I still hadn't made a real commitment to the new church or to God. I had a hard time accepting that a power greater than myself could restore me to sanity—the second step—and it was harder still for me to accept the third step, which asked me to turn my will and life over to the care of God. My ego, which had driven so much of my self-destructive behavior, was still shouting, *I'm a Marine, a martial artist, and an Ironman triathlete. I got into this, and I can get out of it.*

Still, as I sat alone and journaled in front of the fireplace, I often felt the full weight of my behavior over the years—the people I'd hurt, the people I'd offended, my selfishness, my insecurities. At one of my meetings, a guest speaker said something that really scared me.

"When a drunken horse thief sobers up, he's still a horse thief," he said.

Am I just a horse thief, in the end? I wrote those words in my journal that night, with just a little pool of light on the page, and a warmer light from the fire at my feet. I flipped back to the previous pages, the recounting of bullshit I'd done and the bullshit persona I had maintained. Page after page after page. *Is this just who I am?* My chest clenched, and tears poured down my face. I bent in half, my face on my knees, and cried.

Then, a cold nose, investigating my hair. Even through my sobs, I laughed. Dutchess, our aging golden retriever, was my faithful companion through those long sessions of reckoning. I straightened, and she rested her head comfortably in my lap, as if to say, *I feel your pain, and I'm here with you. It's going to be okay.*

I think she may have taught me more about empathy than any human.

I tried to believe Dutchess's assurance that everything would be okay, but it wasn't easy. Only three weeks after the DWI, I was scheduled to lecture at a conference in Orlando, Florida, which had always been a huge party spot for me. I honestly didn't know how I'd handle the temptation. At least I was sleeping soundly for the first time in years—and awakening without a hangover was refreshing. The day I arrived at the conference, I turned in early and got a good night's sleep.

The next morning, as I walked to the lecture hall, I was startled by loud birdsong: I'd never heard birds singing so loudly or beautifully. The notes echoed. It was like listening to an orchestra. My sensory perception seemed to be heightened. I broke into a huge smile, feeling as though I was being treated to a concert by a chorus of angels. The fog of alcohol was clearing, and I was experiencing the "pink cloud," a gift of sobriety showing me how good life could be without booze. For years, I'd sought a high from bottles; now, I was learning I could get high on everyday life.

And yet—and I understand that this emotional roller coaster is typical of early sobriety—by nightfall I was wallowing in self-pity. I knew a lot of my friends were at that moment well into an evening of hard drinking. I'd excused myself by saying I was on an antibiotic and couldn't drink for months. But as I sat in my room, I felt the old familiar restlessness. I decided that instead of ordering room service, I'd grab a bite to eat from the quiet hotel bar.

Welcome to the alcoholic mind.

I walked in looking for an emotional fix—hoping to find people from the conference who'd seen me, who'd be star-struck and treat me like I was something special. But I was disappointed; the place was empty.

As I waited for my order, a guy walked up to my left and ordered a double-malt scotch. Then another guy walked up to my right and ordered a twenty-two-ounce Yuengling. I stared at the bubbles in the golden lager, watching the condensation race down the chilled glass, remembering the cold bitterness of the first sip.

I'm here by myself. Nobody would ever know. Nobody would ever know, Johnny. And then: *What the fuck am I doing?*

I left without getting my food, rushed into my room, and dropped to my knees and prayed. Then I called my sponsor. "I just went down to the hotel bar. 'For a snack,' supposedly, can you *believe*—"

"Slow down. Are you okay? Did you drink?"

"I didn't drink, but Jesus. Jesus. Those words are so loud in my head right now. *I am powerless over alcohol.*"

"Thank God you called me," he said, and his voice was calm but full of feeling. It wasn't an expression—he meant it literally. John: Thank God. "Get on your knees and thank God for keeping you sober. And as soon as you can, go to a meeting."

In a twelve-step program, it always comes back to that. No matter what my problem is, I can call my sponsor, and my sponsor will say: *Go to a meeting; pray. Good thing you called me—call me anytime you need to.* It's very simple formula: Don't drink, say a prayer, go to a meeting. "Hey, but what about this, sponsor, this is a really good problem, really different and interesting!" Same answer: don't drink, say a prayer, go to a meeting. "What if this happens?" Oh, that's a good one. If that happens, don't drink, say a prayer, go to a meeting. It always comes down to those things.

It comes down to those three things because it works.

And still, still—even after that incident, when prayer was the first remedy I turned to—even then, I struggled for weeks with the idea of relinquishing control to God. I spoke to my sister Lisa, who had found comfort in religion. Even though I hadn't talked to her much during the past several years as I sealed myself in my own bubble of selfishness, she was more than happy to share her experience with me. "Things may look bleak now, but if you just turn everything over to God, you'll find peace," she said.

Part of me wanted to believe her, but part of me still felt like this was a little extreme. It just didn't sound real—too dramatic. It didn't sound like me. *I'm not that desperate yet.*

I also called Benji, the music director at The Chapel and now my friend, and he said the same thing. "Turn it over to God," he said. I still wasn't ready.

But toward the end of February 2011, seven weeks after my DWI, the weight of my burdens was suffocating me. I'd walk through my days, doing my job, caring for my children, trying to make things up to Michelle, trying to stay sober. And underneath it all, I still felt uncertain, I still felt guilty, I still felt angry, and I still felt afraid. I felt it, all the pain I'd masked with drinking, and it stirred and boiled inside me as I moved smiling and professional through my day. Sometimes I felt like I was going crazy.

One day, I called a friend from the Marines, Scott, who was a sheriff in Ohio. "Hey, Scott! How you doing?"

The pause on the other end of the line had a weird quality. He said gently, "I don't know if you heard, but I got shot."

My heart skipped, and I moved to close the door of

the room I was in. "What do you mean, you got shot?"

"Went on a domestic abuse call, guy came out with a rifle and shot me in the face." His voice sounded grim, grainy, and distant. "Lost my sight, John. He shot me in the face, and now I'm blind."

I didn't know if I was standing or sitting, I was in so much shock. "What ... how did ... why would a guy ..." I couldn't even get a clear question out.

"He was drunk and on drugs," Scott said, disgust in his voice. "Didn't even know what he did, had no memory of it at all. Woke up in handcuffs. Got thirty years."

After I hung up, all I could think about were those texts I had no memory of writing. Drunk and on drugs. No memory.

The next day, I went to the locked closet where I kept a couple of rifles. I didn't want them in the house anymore. I didn't think I was capable of pulling a gun on someone, and I have never seriously considered suicide. But I was a pressure cooker then; I couldn't trust myself. I took them to the police department and turned them over—"just take them away," I said. The young desk officer took them without further comment.

I was that unsure, in that moment, of where this sobriety thing was going. *Is this just my cute effort to get out of trouble? Am I just doing this to get out of trouble, or do I really want to get sober?*

The fact was, I did not know, and I could not trust myself.

The only peace I found was at the twelve-step meetings. It was like, at the meetings, I had permission to feel all those things. At the meetings, I didn't feel alone, like everyone else had it all together. All my cracks and mistakes and flaws were understood, and were okay.

One night, I was writing in my journal next to the fireplace, Dutchess at my side as always. The fire spit and crackled, my pen scratched across the white page, but otherwise the house was quiet. I wish I could tell you what I was writing about, but I don't remember. I only remember that I was in great pain, overloaded by stress, by fear, by shame and confusion. I felt true mental illness, in that moment. I felt hopeless and powerless and in deep, deep trouble.

Suddenly, I remembered Benji from my church saying, "John, just turn it over to God—get on your knees and surrender."

Whoa, I thought at the time. *That's a little too much, I don't know if I'm ready for that.*

I remembered my sister's warm, low, familiar voice saying the same thing over the phone: "John, just surrender your life to God. Give it up." I'd thought, *Hang on, I'm in a lot of pain, but I don't know if I am that desperate yet. I think I can manage this.*

And all at once, I felt God's presence. And in that moment, when God came to me, I realized: *I can't manage this. I am absolutely going crazy, it's unbearable.* I once heard Benji saying, "God, take this from me."

So I dropped to my knees and said those words aloud: "God, take this all from me, I beg you. All this fear and anxiety, the worry, the frustration, the anger, take it all."

For a moment I thought—*am I doing this right? Is*

this how you do it? Even in that moment, trying to be in control. But then I realized: it's not about what I say, it is not about my words, it's about surrender.

So I surrendered. I begged God to take it from me, take it all—the stress, my fear, my ego. "Take this from me, and I will do anything you say." Tears ran down my face.

I don't know how long I was down on my knees, but my legs were stiff when I finally tried to move.

And when I stood, I stood up a different man. I just wasn't the same. Everything changed, immediately, right there. When I stood up, it was with a sense of purpose: I knew what I had not known before, that it was going to be okay.

It was an absolutely transformative moment in my life, maybe the most transformative of all. I remember now a twelve-step friend telling me he'd been talking to someone in early sobriety, and he said it was like the guy was still fighting, still in the ring with alcohol, and he kept getting knocked down. My friend told him, "Why don't you just stay down, then? Why don't you just not get up? Why don't you just not fight?"

But even though I had found God, the world did not stop spinning. In the midst of all this profound soul-searching, I still had to keep swinging at all life's curveballs. I brought my newfound trust in God with me—but that didn't mean it was easy.

Shortly after that night, I had to meet with the IRS auditor. She saw that there was no way I could justify some of my deductions, and while my accountant readily took the blame, the auditor decided there were enough questions that an audit of my 2008 and 2009 returns was in order.

Meanwhile, prior to the DWI, I'd very publicly promised a patient I'd diagnosed with leukemia that I would run a marathon on her behalf. I was running as part of Team in Training, raising money for the Leukemia and Lymphoma Society.

Following the DWI, training felt impossible. It was all I could do to keep focused on my recovery. I remember during one team session, I was struggling through the run with my mind in overdrive, spewing toxic thoughts. *You can't finish this marathon. You're a piece-of-shit slob, nothing but a joke. You're a pathetic hypocrite. Who do you think you're fooling, Bielinski?*

And then I saw a heavyset woman, a team member, who was struggling more than I was. I immediately wanted to cheer her on. "Hey, you're looking good," I said to her. "Keep it up! You've got this! Don't quit."

A remarkable thing happened. As I tried to motivate this woman, my negative self-talk disappeared. As I would come to see in my sobriety journey, it's when I try to help others that I'm closest to God. In the end, I was able to train well enough to complete the marathon in a respectable time.

I started volunteering at a homeless shelter for four hours a week serving lunch. I knew I couldn't wave a wand and make up for years of selfish behavior, but I wanted to be as close to God as I could while I tried to become a new and better person. I stood behind the food counter, fixing good, full plates of chicken, rolls, and vegetables. Serving these men—they were mostly men, some quiet and hollow-eyed, some joking, some radiating anger and bitterness, all down-and-out—I had the same feeling I had at twelve-step meetings: I am the same as them, the same sore heart, the same sturdy soul. I was grateful to them. Again: blessings flooded in when I got outside myself.

I was attending The Chapel regularly, volunteering, going to twelve-step meetings. And I'd just started a new job as a nighttime house officer at DeGraff Hospital, covering in-house calls under a supervising physician. While I often dealt with critically ill patients, I also had plenty of alone time, thinking and praying all night long. That was perfect, because I was in the process of negotiating the difficult fourth step: taking an exhaustive and unflinching moral inventory of myself.

With my sponsor's guidance, I started by looking at my resentments. I had a lot of them: I had resentments toward Michelle—especially that I felt she wouldn't trust me, wouldn't work with me now, though I also understood why. I had resentments of Dad, for his stiffness and distance, and even of Billy, who was still a drinker, and wasn't happy with my new life. But resentments are toxic to a guy who is trying to clean up his life, and I was able to release my judgments of my father and brother so that our relationships could at least be peaceful, if not close.

I had more serious resentments toward my mother and the Catholic Church. For the church, it had never been a good fit for me. I vividly recall myself as a child, lying alone on the floor of my room reciting the Lord's Prayer: "Our father, who art in heaven, hallowed be thy name ..." and stopping. "What does 'hallowed' even *mean*? What is 'hallowed,' and why do I know this prayer by heart? Why am I repeating this like a parrot? I don't even know what I am saying."

The answer was "to be good," of course, and in my family, that seemed to be the point of church. We went to church, we brought up the offering: Oh, then we are a *good* family. As I grew a little older, Catholicism as I understood it (and my understanding may well have been wrong or incomplete) began to feel like blackmail. And now, as an adult, I could see how harmed I had been by that version of the Catholic Church: Oh my gosh, if I doubt God I am not going to heaven. Oh my gosh, if I masturbate ... It seemed geared toward making people feel guilty and ashamed.

Now I had found a church that taught: it is a journey, and you are forgiven. You are good. I heard a story in church, where Jesus says to a guy—me, say— "John, how are you doing?"

And I have to reply, "Jesus I am not doing so well. I am a sinner, I have lustful thoughts, and I am prideful and I am angry and I've nipped at some people. I am selfish and I'm struggling, Jesus. I'm breaking a lot of the rules, sinning left and right."

Then God says to Jesus: "So how is John doing?"

And Jesus says, "John is perfect. He is exactly where we want him. He is ready for us."

That is my theology now, and I've struggled—still struggle—to overcome my bitterness about my Catholic upbringing. And that mattered in my life, because Michelle is Catholic.

As for my mother, we haven't been able to be around each other much because she still drinks and I feel like there are always tornadoes of drama. I do still have resentment toward her, but I don't cling to it. We are largely estranged—but I am also aware, after all this time, that grownups don't always act the way that kids want them to. I could also see what enormous pain she had been in for so many years.

This was one of the most helpful insights I gained. I could see not just my own pain, but also the pain of others.

And when I looked at the resentments I had acquired as an adult, I began to get the first glimmers that the problem was not with the person I resented, but with me and my reactions: I didn't think Michelle had been as supportive of me as she should have been. What was there for her to support? For all those years, I'd been all about me, me, me. I had emotionally abandoned her in my alcoholism.

I wasn't so surprised by this realization, that I had been an inherently selfish person. What surprised me was seeing the other side of the coin—my fear.

When I remembered my bragging, striving, and egomania, and when I dug down deep and asked where these behaviors had come from, I saw they sprang from feeling like I was not enough. I remembered struggling in school. I remembered feeling dumb. I remembered a family friend's reaction when I told her I planned to be a doctor: *How cute.*

Then I thought about the night Billy was shot. Up until this moment, when I was looking down at my notebook, I would have told anyone who asked that the incident hadn't really affected me much—I hadn't even cried after it happened. But now, remembering it, I put myself back in the moment, seeing Jim raise the gun. Hearing the gun fire: *pop! pop!* Watching Billy fall to the ground. I felt an icy, terrible fear grip my heart. I felt horrified and guilty and shameful that my little brother was shot in front of me, that I hadn't protected him. I *couldn't* have protected him, I argued with myself. It was impossible; I didn't see the gun until it was too late.

Even now, remembering, I was *defending* myself—because I hadn't defended my brother, and no one had defended me. I had sat in a classroom with Jim, my entire body tense with fear and dread, still a child but feeling like now it was me against the world. And since then I'd been fighting and fighting—myself, my doubts, my fears, the world—fighting for control and certainty that I could never truly have, assurance and peace that had to come from within.

Yet again, with Dutchess's loyal head in my lap, I sobbed. I cried the tears that I'd held back for twenty-five years.

The irony of this period was that in order to gain these insights, in order to understand my selfishness, I had to be relentlessly selfish; I had to dwell inside my own mind and spirit to understand how they had become corroded. I had to sit alone by the fire, writing and thinking, for hours.

But the fact was, even when I tried to share my newfound insights with Michelle, she wanted no part of it. She saw I was going to church and twelve-step meetings with enthusiasm, but she didn't want to talk about my journey. She had those walls, and they made me feel so lonely. But why had she built those walls? Because my alcoholism had left her alone long ago.

So there we were, two lonely people, not knowing how to get past those walls we'd made together.

Our relationship had a few bright spots, like the little white mayapple flowers that pop out of the snow in early spring. One day in March, Michelle surprised me, stopping me as I walked into our bedroom, her hand lightly on my chest. It was a moment—she had something to express. She smiled at me—a genuine smile, "I really like who you're becoming," she said, her eyes glistening.

I think her words surprised her as much as me.

A month later, my case came to trial. As Michelle and I arrived in the courtroom, I felt uncomfortable in my suit. It was like I was choking. I had no idea what would happen, not even as my lawyer presented my defense.

He noted my honorable service as a United States Marine and my professional standing. He talked about my still-growing business. And when the arresting officer was on the stand, my lawyer led him through the evening's events.

"Now officer, how many people have you arrested on suspicion of DWI?"

"At least one hundred, maybe more."

"How would you describe my client compared to these other arrests?"

"He was the most respectful person I ever arrested, for DWI or anything else."

I ended up getting the lightest possible punishment on a lesser charge of driving while ability impaired. The judge was convinced I was an otherwise good guy who'd fucked up. My punishment: I had a limited driver's license for six months; I'd only be able to drive to and from work; I'd have to listen to victim impact statements to learn how others had been seriously harmed by drunk drivers; and I'd have to attend DWI school.

I ran a finger underneath my collar. *I'm never going to have to go through this again.* I turned and nodded to Michelle, my knees wobbling a little. I was being given the gift of a second chance. I remember hearing country wisdom: "If you fuck up and work hard, you fucked up. But if you fuck up and fuck up, then you're a fuck-up!" I was going to work hard—very hard.

There was a lot going on in the aftermath of my DWI, but I was still managing to grow my business. Because I wasn't drinking, I had more time for everything, even with all the new things I was tackling as part of my recovery. I was more present. In fact, not drinking meant I was gaining productivity on two levels. I now had extra time: not only the time I'd previously spent drinking, but also the time that had been absorbed with my hangovers.

It was around this time that I approached the Masons about resuming the process of joining their organization. Understandably, they were hesitant: I had bailed on them before. How many bites did they think I got at this apple?

But they were kind enough to let me explain that I wanted to be with these men not to put another line on my resume but to serve others—and not to serve others so I could beat my chest and brag about what a good guy I am. I'd withdrawn from the Masons before because I didn't think I was an honorable man. Now I wanted in because, though imperfect, I wanted to be like them. With great generosity, they welcomed me back at the lodge, and within the year I was raised to the level of Master Mason.

Even today, I understand I may stumble. But I also know that surrounding myself with godly, spiritual men can only help me along the way. The Masons are not a merit badge. Like my twelve-step program, they're a lifeline.

By September 2011, I felt like I was gaining understanding in many areas of my life. The sermons at church, along with my discussions at twelve-step meetings and with the Masons, were filling me with insights and hope. But when I tried to share with Michelle, she stiff-armed me. She may have told me she'd liked who I was becoming, but she didn't want the details. As a couple, we were taking the proverbial two steps forward, one step back. Intellectually, I understood that it would take time to regain her trust. I'd neglected her and cheated her of my presence for years, and it would be unreasonable to expect her to let down her defenses in just a few months. And though I no longer felt she was just looking for an excuse to kick me out of the house, I also knew our relationship was still strained.

Michelle wasn't used to my trying to work through our problems. In the past, we would become passive-aggressive and maybe yell a bit, and then I would leave and go drink. Now, I stuck around and did my best to work it out. But Michelle didn't like that. Looking back, I wonder if she felt I was trying to manipulate her—given my track record, it's hard to blame her. But at the time, I wondered whether we truly had a future.

It was unbelievably difficult: whenever I tried to talk to my wife about issues with real weight—spirituality, goals, how we can best synergize our parenting—I'd be met with "I don't want to talk about this God stuff. I don't want to hear it." I found that very difficult.

During one of our fights, she said, "You know what? I hate your twelve-step meetings. In fact, I liked you better when you were drinking."

I felt the blood rush to my face. My fists clenched involuntarily. But instead of lashing out, as I would have done a year earlier, I took a deep breath. She didn't mean that, I told myself. The pain I'd caused her through the years was deep and real, and my recovery was just as confusing for her as it was for me.

When I stopped drinking, many things changed, and change was difficult to deal with, even if it was for the better. I'd learned as I worked through my steps that it was best to let those kinds of remarks go without comment; it wouldn't help to reply with words lined with barbed wire.

I continued to work through the steps. I admitted my wrongs to God and to my sponsor. I got myself ready to let those character defects go and to ask God to remove them.

I reflected on what Kim had told me months ago,

though it seemed like years ago: when he embarked on a life of sobriety, he'd changed not only his behavior, but his friends. The first few days after my DWI, I thought I'd still be running around with Billy and Trevor—I just wouldn't drink. I promised myself that if anyone tried to tempt me into drinking, I'd smack them across the face. But the fact of the matter is, that toward the end of my drinking days, I drank mostly by myself. It wasn't about being sociable. It was about numbing my pain and quieting my racing mind.

But my old drinking behavior absolutely stopped. I didn't have time to hang around people getting drunk. I was too busy trying to get myself right with myself— and with Michelle, Johnny, Sarah, and Matthew.

There were times during the first year that were very uncomfortable. When Matthew's hockey season began that fall, I was again around the other kids' dads. I'd had a reputation as a heavy drinker, and I was good buddies with another drink-pounding dad named Mike. But this year, I wasn't drinking. During one tournament, I stood near the concession stand between periods. I was wearing a Masons sweatshirt and sipping a hot chocolate when Mike approached.

He looked at my drink and sneered. "That's not going to put hair on your chest. You should at least put some Schnapps in it." He glanced at my sweatshirt. "But I guess now that you're a Mormon, you won't drink anymore."

"I'm a Mason, you stupid fuck. Not the same thing."

That Christmas of 2011, as I neared the one-year anniversary of my sobriety, was the first Christmas in years that was joyful for me. On the surface, it may not have looked very different from past Christmases. But this Christmas, I wasn't a bystander sucking down beers on the couch while everyone else celebrated. I helped decorate the tree, and I set up a train to run around the base of the tree, just like my mom had for Lisa, Billy, and me so many years before. And now, for the first time, I understood what Christmas was all about: Jesus's birthday was a kind of promise. That darkest time of year was kind of like a twelve-step meeting: no one had to pretend to be happy, no one had to fake it. We all gathered together, as the broken people we are, and in that honest, loving gathering was peace, and more than peace: a light, a shining child, God's gift breaking through our broken darkness: the light of love.

For years, Michelle, the kids, and I had spent New Year's Eve with some other families. We took turns hosting, ringing in the New Year with booze, the guests then spending the night. That year, I think my not drinking made the others a little uncomfortable, but I didn't care. I woke up the next day, the first day of 2012, feeling wonderful.

A few days later was my first sobriety anniversary. I had asked Michelle if she would come to a meeting to present me with my one-year coin, but she was still wary of becoming involved. She was happy that the program seemed to be working for me, and she was becoming more supportive when she could see by my behavior that I wasn't just trying to bullshit everyone. But the twelve-step group wasn't for her.

It had been a rough but good year. I'd made it through eight of the twelve steps, ending with making a list of all the people I had harmed—not a short list, but for every name on it I felt a specific kind of shame and sadness. I emerged from the year with a better understanding of myself than I'd had going in, that was for sure. I had found a measure of peace. I could sit on the couch with a cup of coffee and feel a deep, tangible contentment. The demons that had haunted me the previous year had fled. I was sleeping through the night.

I'd also been able to come to grips with my illness. I wasn't ashamed of it anymore, though I was sensitive to the power of the word *alcoholic*. To some, it's a vulgar word. So I framed it a different way: I live in sobriety from alcohol.

I felt like I'd survived a terminal illness, like I'd been given another shot. And with that came the understanding that I could never again take anything for granted. I learned to appreciate the day for the day.

At the same time, I knew I had a lot of work to do. While Michelle and I had reached a kind of a truce, I missed a sense of intimacy and support, and our spiritual lives still weren't in sync; she continued to go to Catholic Mass and didn't want to hear anything about my nondenominational Christian services. The business was good, but it could be better. I still wasn't sure what would come of the IRS audit. Most of all, I knew I was one moment of weakness away from tearing down the new life I'd spent the whole year building. I headed into the New Year with hope and trepidation.

It was time to make amends to those I'd wronged.

Chapter 13

Atonement

Name after name, my list grew—the list of the people I'd harmed with my alcoholic behavior. I remembered in vivid detail how I'd wounded them with a careless word here, a selfish or self-serving act there. It was like watching a documentary of my life—scene after scene showing my failures in high definition. Most of the worst are in the earlier pages of this book.

It was humbling to look at the wreckage I'd caused, and it was scary as hell to think about facing everyone I'd harmed and making amends. But that's what step nine required me to do: make amends to the people I'd harmed wherever possible, except when to do so would injure them or others.

I didn't have to do it alone. My sponsor, with his firm and gentle guidance, helped me understand there were some things I couldn't compensate people for without causing them further hurt. To give examples here from my own life would only cause those people the pain I am trying to avoid.

My sponsor also helped me realize it would be impossible to make amends with *everyone*. There were people—like a man who had once yelled furiously at me on a flight to Vegas, clearly disturbed by my drunkenness—whom I could only remember and feel sorry for having bothered, hurt, or disturbed. All I could do was gather up those memories and loose ends and use them as motivation to stay on the right path.

Even so, I had a daunting number of people to get right with—but I didn't hesitate. One by one I contacted them and explained my situation. The script for each meeting or call was the same: "I know what I did to you or what I believe I did to you," I would say, "but I don't know how it affected you, and if you would like to share with me how my behavior affected you, I would like to hear it." And then I would listen.

My former teaching colleagues were exceptionally gracious. Again and again I told my story, recalling the times I'd acted badly, and I asked what I could do to make things right. Inevitably, people said something along the lines of what my former program director did: "Wow, I didn't know you had these struggles. I'm glad you're turning your life around."

But some amends were more difficult to make. I visited my mother one weekend to try to make amends. But she just kept pouring herself another drink and changing the subject.

I also went to the program director whose teaching

program I had disrespected with my drunken emails and texts. I acknowledged to her fully what I had done, and said, "I am struggling with alcohol, and I'm going through the twelve steps. I wanted to clear the slate and tell you how sorry I am, and what I am doing to make sure I never behave that way again."

Her response was polite and seemed reasonably warm, but I walked out of that building and into the bright, chilly springtime sun feeling unsettled. I was looking for a teaching position at the time, and prospective employers would have had to contact her. Had I unconsciously been looking for what sobriety groups call "secondary gain"—some benefit to myself that would spoil the blessing of making amends selflessly? I went to my sponsor immediately, and we talked it through. The truth is, I should have talked through my motivation with him before going. People making amends often lack discernment that way: I should have checked with my sponsor first.

Of all those sessions, I most remember calling Tricia and asking her whether we could meet so I could try to make amends.

She was silent. "No," she said finally. "I don't think I want to do that."

But a little while later, she called back. "I talked it over with Chris," she said, "and he convinced me I should meet with you." I smiled—her husband, Chris, had always been fair and kind to me.

We met at a Tim Hortons for coffee. Sitting at the small laminate table, I looked Tricia in the eyes. "I know what happened, and I know what I did," I said. "But I don't know how it affected you, and I'd like to hear it."

Tricia broke our gaze and looked over my shoulder. "I know you married me out of a sense of obligation," she said, "but I really loved you." She paused. "It really hurt me not to have that love returned."

"I'm sorry," I said. "But I know that doesn't make up for what I did. Is there anything I can do to make this better?"

She thought for a moment. "You could give me more money."

My face flushed and my stomach knotted. I tried not to show my anger—I had *always* met my financial obligations when it came to supporting Johnny. When I got a raise, Tricia got a raise. No fucking way was she getting more money.

A wry smile spread across her face. "Gotcha," she said.

Tricia always did have a sense of humor.

"Now I'm married to a good man who loves me and Johnny," she went on. "I've got a good life. Listen, I'm glad we had this talk and you're taking care of yourself."

We found peace, and I was thankful for that. Step nine was a true blessing to me. I was able to clean up some of the wreckage I'd left in my wake. I was straight with the house. I felt like I was slowly emptying out the bag of rocks I'd been carrying all these years.

Yet the heaviest rock still hung around my neck. I wanted to make amends with Michelle—but she didn't seem like she was in any rush for this to happen. She brushed me off a few times when I tried to have the conversation with her. At last I decided to be very clear. One day, when my wife was sitting on the couch in the living room reading a magazine, I sat down next to her.

"Michelle," I said, "I am ready to make amends to you at any time."

She set down her magazine on an overstuffed cushion. Dust specks hung in a ray of light streaming through a window. Although only a few moments passed, time seemed to stretch into eternity with her silence.

"The thing is," she said finally, "I'm not sure I want to hear what you have to say."

I just kept listening, waiting for her to continue.

"Besides," she said slowly, "I'd rather *see* how you're different now. I'd rather see for myself how you've changed."

Part of me understood. My time in the twelve-step program had taught me that everyone had his or her own battles, burdens, and scars. I wanted Michelle to tell me how my behavior had affected her, and she *was* telling me—in her own way, without saying a word. She didn't need to hear me talk anymore. She'd had a front-row seat to my bullshit for years. What she needed was for me to be the man she'd married.

But at the same time, her stonewalling—not just at this moment, but all the time—hurt a lot. It was far more than not allowing me to progress. I often felt that she was actively pulling me under.

Around this time, one Saturday night, Dutchess had a neurological event—a seizure. The sounds woke me at three in morning, and I scrambled to where she lay by the fireplace, muscles contracting, head drawn back unnaturally. "Dutchess," I said, and knelt beside her.

I was so thankful to be sober that night. Had I been drunk, I could never have made the instant decision to go to the vet. She was a heavy dog, and had I been drunk, I could never have carried her down to the car. I could never have accepted the vet's terrible words: She needs to be put down tonight. And I could never have been present for my family, afterward, if I'd been drunk.

Dutchess was such a good dog. I still miss her every day.

Throughout my transformation and recovery, I'd continued going to church services at The Chapel. I loved hearing the joyous, spirit-moving music from Benji and his band, and when I listened to the pastor's messages, I often felt like he was speaking directly to me. Michelle and the kids didn't come to The Chapel with me often—only on Christmas and Father's Day. Michelle could see how much my church meant to me, but she had a hard time accepting that this was a *real* church—she was still devoted to Catholicism, holding fast to the rituals she'd grown up with—the ones I still resented.

But on the day I was baptized, my family came to be with me.

For a long time, I'd thought it was kind of strange when people my age got dunked up there in front of everyone, and I usually felt uncomfortable watching. But I talked through some of my reservations with the pastor and Benji, and eventually I grew drawn to the idea of professing my faith in this way: making a conscious decision to surrender to God. By now I understood what it meant to surrender to a higher power, and I appreciated the symbolism and importance of baptism as a way of expressing my surrender.

So, on a sun-drenched summer Sunday in the second year of my recovery, I gathered with other church members behind the altar, draped in a bright white garment. Among the three thousand people in attendance that day were Michelle, our kids, and my dad.

I was one of the last people called to the sanctuary, and as I waited, I felt a wave of nerves. Then those nerves disappeared, and I was filled with such an indescribable happiness that I didn't even feel the floor beneath my feet. I felt so sure in that moment that despite all my faults, and despite all the pain I'd caused so many people, God loved me and always would, no matter what.

Finally, I heard my name called and came out into the sanctuary. Seeing all those people there, smiling for me, was a little like driving at night, deep in the pitch-black Nevada desert, and then suddenly seeing Las Vegas expand on the horizon, a glittering pool of light: something so much bigger than me was going on.

But unlike with Vegas, where not much lies beyond the glittering light, here I knew I stood on a foundation of unconditional love.

As I took in the sight of the congregation, I heard a whoop from the music section—Benji was cheering me on. Tears streamed down my cheeks.

Afterward, Michelle and the kids hugged me. Dad, standing awkwardly, finally stepped forward and shook my hand. "I'm not sure why you did this," he said, "but I'm proud of you."

. . .

In a movie, this story would close with me dripping wet, beaming. The end—John lives happily ever after. But a person's life, even a life spent following Christ, isn't so neat and tidy.

About two months after I was baptized, I was speaking at a conference in Raleigh, North Carolina, and something odd happened. As the first day wore on, I felt more and more uneasy, as if I were adrift in a vast sea with no mooring. The old John crept up behind me, then slipped inside. Where was the praise? Where were the admirers? How could I make that happen? It was as if my former self had given me a quick transfusion of bleak, hungry emptiness—and that emptiness needed to be filled.

What I *didn't* feel was the presence of God. I was entering a spiritual desert.

I was frightened—but I didn't run to the bar or try to find other ways of filling the void I felt. Instead, I doubled down on my prayers, even when it felt like they had already dissolved into nothingness by the time they left my lips. The world felt like a bigger, colder place now. I started having doubts. *Is all of this—God, church, even the twelve-step program—is it all just bullshit? What the hell am I doing? Does any of this have any meaning?*

It was horrible. I returned from the conference, and it didn't go away. I was restless, irritable, frustrated. At a twelve-step meeting, a friend named Frank asked me how I was doing.

"Good, everything's good," I said listlessly.

"No it's not," he said. "Don't you try pulling that one on me. I can see something's bothering you." He nodded over my shoulder. "There's your sponsor. Go talk about it."

Balancing a paper cup of sharp, bitter coffee, I approached my sponsor. "Got a minute?"

"Of course," he said, nodding at the empty seat next to him.

I sat down and stared into my coffee cup. "I feel lost," I confessed. "Sometimes I think all of this is just bullshit. *All* of it," I said, waving a hand around the room. "These meetings. God. The Bible. I just—I don't even feel God anymore."

My sponsor nodded. "Why don't you ask God about it?"

So I did—I kept at it. I kept praying, I kept going to church, and I kept attending meetings even though I didn't want to. And slowly, over the next two months, that feeling of desolation lifted.

Now I've accepted that these ebbs and flows are part of my life—periods of peace followed by times when I feel fucking pissed off. I know I just need to have humility and keep working.

I always thought sobriety would look like a line going up and up, steady progress, but now I know it's a jagged line: I'll have some growth, and then I'll stumble and fall on my ass. I've learned to release expectations. I try to stay humble; I know I'm one misstep away from undoing my hard work. I've tried to cultivate what I call *sobrenity*—sobriety and serenity—when it comes to being at peace with the ups and downs.

These same principles of sobriety—humility and hard work no matter what—have helped me grow my business beyond what I ever imagined was possible. Looking back, I see that when I started following Christ, I started doing pretty well in business. Why? I believe it's because I've worked every day to be honest, fair, and transparent in all aspects of my life, business included. I'm trying my best to operate for the good of all, not just myself. This business isn't just about me.

Very quickly, I was able to pay off my loans from my dad and Billy. My *cha-ching!* phone alert for every sale became so annoying that I had to shut it off.

A business coach I hired told me that an hour of uninterrupted work time was equivalent to 2.6 hours of working with interruptions. I started paying attention to how, when I was working at home, I got distracted petting our cat—or I'd suddenly notice the kitchen sink was filled with dirty dishes.

Once I'd noticed how divided my attention was at home, I got an office outside the house. Eliminating those distractions allowed me to focus on business. I was more productive, and the business grew. Michelle got involved on the financial side of things, and her cautious nature proved to be a huge asset. I would see $50,000 in the bank and think, *Woo hoo! Let's get a new car!* But then Michelle would remind me that almost half that money would go to the government in taxes.

I researched different ways to market our products. I studied ads and eye tracking; I studied social media; I learned about influence. The business grew and grew.

Three years in, I hired a business manager who could take some responsibilities off my plate, freeing me up to work on what I was most passionate about:

teaching and content. I took personal development classes and worked on innovative ways to grow CME4LIFE. I figured out that we were only reaching about 25 percent of PA students with our emergency medicine content, whereas if we got into board review, we could reach 100 percent of students.

So I set about to learning everything I could about board review and creating the most engaging, memorable, unique content I could. I remembered the revelation from Johnny's Angels—that helping others learn and have fun learning was my own gift. When the days got long, I took a lesson from my Ironman training: put in the work, day after day, grind it out, and you'll get there. And the boy who'd once been terrified to read aloud in class worked on his delivery and references, fine-tuning gestures and timing, and told stories that hooked the crowds.

Most of all, I held close what I knew from my twelve-step meetings and from church: that when I focused on serving others with humility, not trying to make it all about applause and admiration for me, my own troubles faded away.

The first year that we hit one million in revenue, I was amazed—and then the next year, our revenue was $2.4 million. It took me back to my first belt ceremony in tae kwon do, the "Well done" from my *sa boo nim*, and running to my sister: *I've found something I'm good at.*

So humility and hard work have helped my business—and they've also helped my parenting. Once I got sober, I made it my first priority to be a responsible, reliable parent. I knew I had let down my kids in the past, and I never wanted to let them down again. I never wanted them to see that kind of behavior from me again—and I certainly never wanted to see that behavior in them.

On a trip to Disneyworld, about three years into my sobriety, I found Johnny drunk. He was nineteen at the time, underage—but what was even worse, he had given alcohol to fourteen-year-old Matthew. I flew into a rage, incredulous that this was happening. It was almost a spot intervention: I had to show him in every way at my disposal that this was absolutely unacceptable.

I don't care at all about being my kid's friend. I will be their father, whatever that takes. First I pause, check my motives to make sure they're healthy—and if they are, I won't hesitate to be firm with my kids. They need to know about the dangers of alcohol and drugs, and thank God I am in the position to tell them firsthand.

But I didn't leave it at that first instance of angry discipline. When we returned home, I worked to follow up in a way that was proactive and caring. In many ways, my past is a gift; I feel that what I've been through allows me to bring more empathy and wisdom to tough conversations. I wanted Johnny to really hear what I had to say.

Michelle and I went over to see Tricia and Chris, and we staged a more proper intervention with Johnny. We told him what it did to us and how we felt to see him drinking that way. "You have the genes of an alcoholic," I told Johnny sincerely, "and that means you're prone to alcoholism, too." He was quiet, thoughtful.

Johnny told me later that this intervention had really meant something to him—he had heard what we said to him. I appreciated that, and I took pride in Johnny's progress. I am so proud of my children. When Matthew cracks me up—like when he stomps upstairs from the basement, cursing the whole time, to give me my mandatory goodnight hug—I feel proud. When Sarah shows her kindness—like when I visited my grandmother in a nursing home and found Sarah comforting a crying elderly woman in the hallway—I feel proud. I'm grateful that sober living has allowed me to guide and care for my children.

And so, almost four years into my sobriety, I found myself flourishing in business. I found myself acting as a responsible, loving, effective parent. After realizing how vital it was to my lecturing for me to be physically fit, I had prioritized my health and gotten back into shape. I was practicing my faith devotedly. Sometimes, going to bed at night, I felt actually *giddy*—I was going to sleep with a clear conscience, a sober man, and I would wake up feeling bright and hopeful about the new day.

There was only one area in my life where I still felt like I was stuck.

Michelle would still not open up to me; there was no getting close to her. Things were *better* between us, but there was still distance. We weren't in sync spiritually—she seemed glad The Chapel was working well for me, but she never wanted to hear about services or my thoughts on the Bible. Simple parenting decisions became a power struggle; when I suggested that the kids should do chores, Michelle seemed to take it as a personal insult, like I was criticizing the way she'd raised our children.

But more than anything, I was just profoundly lonely. I often talked to my sponsor about it. Michelle would come home from work, and we could talk—but only as long as it was entirely superficial, household logistics, what happened at work, that kind of thing. Later in sobriety, people understand better—as I now understand better—that my sobriety isn't for me: my sobriety is for my kids, for my family, for the people who work for me. I am sober so I can be of service.

But early on, you're not there yet. Your sobriety is self-focused, it has to be, because you have to be so conscious: don't drink today, go to a meeting, call your sponsor, do the next right thing. Enormous spiritual growth is taking place inside you, day by day. And Michelle wanted nothing to do with any of it, didn't want to hear a word about it.

In my second year of sobriety, I said to myself: *Okay, I've got to find a way to live happily in spite of my marriage.* That sucks to say, but that was where we were. So I signed up for some Anthony Robbins conferences, thinking I could find the happiness in myself, without her. I really like Robbins—he doesn't preach God, but there's a spiritual quality to his work; he elevates the material plane.

Robbins talked about the six basic human needs— you can look them up if you're interested. They're paradoxical: we need certainty and comfort, but we need variety; we need significance, to feel important, but we also need love and connection.

As he talked, I had a realization: My alcoholism had forced Michelle to serve my needs, constantly, unrelentingly, and no one was there to serve hers.

I came home on fire to serve her needs. I tried to talk to her about it, to get her to give me a sense of how I could best do that, but she shut me down.

So I hired a master woodcrafter to create something for me—a kind of wall-mounted abacus, about two feet by four feet, of thick, heavy oak—a beautiful piece of work. The three slides were labeled: certainty at one end, uncertainty at the other; significance on one end, love and connection at the other; growth on one end, contribution on the other. And I had him engrave it to Michelle.

I gave it to her for Christmas that year. Opening it, she was understandably puzzled. I sat by her side, while the kids at our feet played and shouted amid mounds of wrapping paper.

"This is so you don't have to talk to me," I said. "Do you see? You can help me know what your needs are, any day, without having to say a word." I slid the marker closer to *significance*, then closer to *love and connection*, to show her.

I felt her shoulders tensing up, so I kept talking, more and more anxiously. "Help me know how I am serving you, Michelle. Help me know when you need more certainty, help me know when you need more excitement in our marriage. You don't have to tell me! Just show me every once in a while. We won't have to talk about it—I know you're not ready for that. I can just see—'ah, she's not feeling loved'—and turn up the heat a little, like that."

She didn't look at me, just slid one of the sliders back and forth with her finger for a moment, absently. "Well ... thanks," she said finally, and turned to open another present.

She hung it up, but she never used it. Not once. It broke my heart. I was trying so hard—maybe too hard. Maybe I didn't have the inner strength and security to simply wait and keep working for more years, to keep trying to meet her needs without ever knowing if I was hitting the mark. One day, months later, I took it down in a moment of anger. "Listen," I said, carrying it off to the garage. "If you don't think this is important, that's no different than when I was living alcoholically."

It went on like that for two or three years. I would come home from church, giddy to share life-changing insights, and would be met with a stiff arm: *Don't bring that to me, I don't want this.*

As I approached my third anniversary of sobriety, I thought I would honor my new understanding of service by going on a medical mission trip. So in January 2014, on the anniversary itself, I took Michelle to a four-star restaurant in Buffalo, excited to share my plans. "I want to donate some time to provide medical services in a poor country."

She exploded. "No! No, you are not going, you *can't.*" It turned into a raging fight. We had to leave the restaurant. My third anniversary of sobriety ended with her getting out of the car sobbing, and me driving away in a hot fury to find a twelve-step meeting.

The night I got my DWI, Michelle was on the brink, teetering between staying and going. Now it was me who was on the brink—I knew we both deserved a better life than this together. I wanted us to honor one another better.

And God, I was lonely.

We had both been wounded, and I didn't know if we could heal.

Chapter 14

Fork in the Road

One afternoon in June 2015, I took Matthew, then fourteen years old, to see *Avengers: Age of Ultron*, a Marvel superhero movie. He was all fired up for it, and I was excited, too.

As we drove past a stand of flowering dogwoods, their white petals fluttering in the sun, my phone rang—Michelle. I turned off the radio and put the phone to my ear. "Hey," I said cheerfully. "What's up?"

Her voice was tight and cold. She was angry with me about something—and instantly, with shocking force, the rage and loneliness inside me rose up to meet hers. Clearly, we were about to have the fight we'd been waiting years to have: a cataclysmic, possibly marriage-ending fight.

"*Wait*," I snapped. "I'm bringing Matt home right now. We'll talk in person." Clicking END CALL, I dropped the phone and made a furious U-turn.

I felt Matt's eyes on me, and my face grew hot. "I'm sorry, buddy," I said, trying to keep my voice calm and even. "We're gonna have to see the movie another time, okay?" He nodded sadly—he knew something was up.

Back at the house, I told Michelle, "Come with me."

"Where?" she said tersely.

"Somewhere we can talk," I said in a low voice, then called over my shoulder, "Matt, hold down the fort. We'll be back soon." Without a word, white-lipped—as white-lipped as I probably was myself—Michelle followed me out to the car.

For fifteen minutes we drove in taut silence. I had no idea where I was going. We passed the stand of dogwoods again; they looked like a dirty bedsheet to me now.

A few minutes later, I realized that the car had brought us within a block of The Chapel. I pulled in to the vast, empty lot and parked.

Michelle sat with her arms crossed, staring blankly through the windshield. I could feel the heat coming off her. I felt angry, too, and a whole ugly nest of other miserable feelings, like shame and loneliness and fear—but I also felt something else, something that surprised me: relief.

"Good," I said. "I'm glad it's come to this." As I said the words, they surprised me, but I knew they were true. "Now let's talk. Now let's really talk about our marriage."

Michelle turned to me, her face struggling between fury and pain. When she spoke, it was like a punch to my face. In the long minutes that followed, we both said things we'd been needing to say for too long.

I am not going to describe what we said here, or the details of what our fight was about. I withhold that information not to protect myself—at this point, that's the last thing I want to do—but to protect my wife and my family. It's like the warning in twelve-step programs about the "making amends" step: I won't make myself vulnerable at the expense of those I've already hurt too much.

But I will tell you that I sat in the front seat of our SUV at the edge of a church parking lot, and opened up all my rage and pain to her, and she did the same.

After how long—twenty minutes? thirty? more?—we were closing in on something like truth. "I can't do it anymore," I said. I was near tears. "I can't, Michelle. I can't be so isolated in my marriage. I am so thankful for this fight. I am so fucking thankful. Because if you feel like you've given me everything you can, and you're being the best wife you can be—then that's it. I'm packing my bags tonight." I pounded the steering wheel with the heel of my hand. "Because if this is all our marriage is, I'm fucking *done*."

It was like the night of my DWI, except now it wasn't Michelle who was at the brink in our marriage— it was me.

Michelle uncrossed her arms and looked at me with wide, furious eyes. "*You're* done?" she shot back. "After everything you put us through, for years and years and years—and you're the one who's done?"

The car was becoming suffocating. Glancing around to make sure no one was near enough to hear us,

I rolled my window down. Cool air swept into the car.

"If you'd left me the night I called you from the police station," I said, "no one could blame you, least of all me. If you'd left me one of the many, many nights I came home reeking of alcohol, fair enough." I looked at her pale face, the set of her mouth, the way the sudden breeze had tangled her hair against her cheek. "But for three years, I have fought to pull myself out of that place. And for three years, you've treated me like a piece of shit. It's like you cannot see that I'm not a piece of shit anymore."

Michelle opened her mouth to respond, then closed it. She blinked, and I could see she was trembling on some edge, trying to make a decision, like a bird deciding whether or not to trust the air.

"I want to pray," I said. Suddenly my anger had dropped away—not vanished, but slipped into the background, the way if you saw your child drowning, the fear would fall back to let you swim with all your strength. I thought: *We will save our marriage in this moment, or it will die.*

"I want to pray, Michelle," I repeated. "Please: Will you pray with me?"

And she agreed. To my astonishment, to her great credit, and by the grace of God, she nodded her head. And for the first time in our lives, we prayed together. It was a private prayer, a broken, tearful prayer, between us and God, and I won't share it here. But I can tell you it was a deep, deep blessing.

. . .

In all my worst days, Michelle had never walked away, and she didn't on that day, and neither did I. Slowly, we began to repair our relationship. Michelle showed a real interest in spending more time with me; I suddenly had a lot more patience. Shortly after our talk in the church parking lot, Michelle came with me to a conference—something she had rarely done in recent years. After my lecture, she came up to me wearing a funny expression, looking a little startled.

"What's that face about?" I asked.

"It's just …" she said. "You've gotten *really* good. Holy cow."

I grinned. Michelle had never been one to throw compliments around. The rest of that weekend, whenever I wasn't lecturing, Michelle and I spent time together and talked—really *talked*—about our marriage, our hopes, and our aspirations.

I tried to explain to Michelle why I'd never felt comfortable with Catholicism—that feeling that I was just going through the motions or that my questions weren't supposed to be asked. I felt like Catholicism was trying to blackmail me with God's grace: I could earn it, but only if I played by their rules. I understand that many people have found God's presence through the Catholic Church, and I know that many find comfort in its rituals. It just isn't right for me. But I'd made my breakthrough at The Chapel, and I wanted Michelle to experience what I'd discovered there.

Michelle started coming to The Chapel with me and bringing the kids. She even talked to me about the sermons sometimes, and we prayed together more often.

I'm happy that Michelle now thinks of The Chapel as *our* church, and I love knowing that we're growing spiritually together.

I've heard it said that two components of a successful business are marketing and innovation—making yourself appealing to people, and offering something new. I think the same is true with relationships. We need to keep appealing to each other, and we need to keep growing and exploring.

As she began to allow herself to trust me, Michelle became more willing to step outside her comfort zone in other ways, as well. She started working out with a trainer, which was a big deal because her mantra had always been "Sure, I'll work out—as long as I don't have to sweat." She even agreed to get scuba certified so that we could scuba dive on a family vacation to the Bahamas. Before, she would have dismissed an unfamiliar idea like that—but now she surprised me by being game.

During that first scuba dive, I was astonished by the peace and beauty of the underwater world. I moved with my wife and children through the crystal-clear water, exploring sunken ships and coral reefs. At one point, twelve-year-old Sarah—who was Michelle's dive partner—got distracted and didn't realize that Michelle wasn't with us. The dive instructors left me, Matthew, and Sarah to go and investigate. It turned out that Michelle had been taking in too much air and had bobbed to the surface, where she was struggling in choppy water. Before, she might have been angry and resentful, but now she handled it with grace: "I'm fine," she said when we came up to the surface to check on her. "Just a little shaken up." I smiled at her.

We also worked on recognizing our triggers. We all have them—those little things that set us off. Maybe it's someone cutting us off on the freeway. Maybe it's when the newspaper gets tossed in the bushes instead of on the porch. In a marriage, triggers can get truly mundane—hair in the sink, forgetting to close a drawer.

When we're triggered, our brains get hijacked, ordering a flood of chemicals into our systems that produce the familiar fight-or-flight response—or in my case, the fight-or-fight response. Even under the best of circumstances, if we walk away from the fight, it takes a good twenty minutes for these chemicals to get cleared out from our system.

Armed with this insight, I suggested to Michelle that when we started to get into an argument, either one of us could "call Wii"—we could demand a videogame challenge as an alternative to arguing. She smiled and shook her head wryly. "Sure," she said. "Why not?"

So one day, when we somehow irritated each other at the same time, I rushed to grab a game controller. "Wii!" I shouted.

"Are you crazy?" she said angrily.

"We have to try it," I said, just as angry as she was. "Sword fighting!"

She picked up her own controller, and we funneled our frustrations into the game, swinging our virtual swords furiously. I felt my anger melting into sheer exertion, movement without any emotion. Twenty minutes later, we collapsed on the couch, laughing hysterically—although I was pissed she'd won. I tousled Michelle's hair. This was progress.

This kind of progress in our marriage took work and attention—just like sobriety. Steps ten to twelve of the twelve-step program are the maintenance steps. I will never *complete* the steps. I will just keep on working and doing my best.

The tenth step is continuing to take personal inventory and promptly admitting wrongdoing. This kind of maintenance requires intense honesty from me. If there is any shit in my life, I have to clean it up right away. Sometimes I might make a careless, heat-of-the-moment remark to Michelle, say something without thinking. If I hear that voice in my head saying I was wrong, I have to own it immediately. "I'm sorry," I'll say quickly. "I spoke just now without thinking. Let's start over again." This keeps conflict from building up; it helps me stay on the right path.

At the end of each day, I examine whether there's anything I need to clean up—a case of dishonesty here, a selfish or self-seeking behavior there—that I didn't catch in the moment. My sponsor put it best: he told me that when he was growing up, a circus would come to town, led by a procession of elephants. Right behind the elephants came a group of clowns with shovels and garbage cans on rollers. He asked his dad what the clowns were doing. "Just watch, son," his dad told him. When the elephants lifted their tails and dropped huge craps in the street, the clowns quickly scooped it up and tossed it in the cans.

"That's what step ten is," my sponsor said. "If you shit on your life, you have to clean it up right away, even if it's embarrassing."

The eleventh step is to pray and meditate to know God's will and have the strength to carry it out. It's a lot harder than it sounds.

I resisted the impulse to get a tattoo when I was in the Marines. I didn't even get one after I completed the Ironman. So I was surprised when I kept having visions of a tattoo while I was praying to know God's will and carry it out. *What? God wants me to get a tattoo?* In the spring of 2014, I got one, a large and unmistakable cross on my leg.

I still wrestle with that. Was it just an identity claim? Was getting a tattoo really God's will, or just another ego-based move? I can't really know. But now it's a permanent part of me, a symbol of my salvation, and it's not going anywhere. Trying to know God's will is a struggle for me, and I'm sure it will always be difficult. All I can do is get quiet and pray.

The twelfth step asks me to carry this message to other alcoholics and practice these principles in all my affairs. Early on in my sobriety, I tried talking to drunks drying out at the hospital, but that didn't work so well; alcoholics will tell you anything to get you off their backs. Now, when I feel called to, I'll try to connect with someone struggling. I'll say, "Believe it or not, some of the most honorable men and women I know have gone through what you're going through right now." It's a way of giving people hope—helping them understand that their struggle has value. It's hard to feel like you're doing a great job carrying out step twelve—it always feels like you could be doing more.

At one of my meetings, I described my frustration about carrying the message to others. "I just don't feel like I'm doing this very well," I confessed. "I struggle with trying to carry the message—maybe I don't have the message yet."

"You're mistaken," one man at the table said. I looked at him with surprise. He said, "You've helped me tremendously with the things that you say."

"Me, too," another man chimed in. "You've really helped me, too."

You just never know the kind of impact you can have. I'm not convinced I can do anything more than live the twelve steps, and I'm happy it seems to show. It's not uncommon now when I've finished a lecture for someone to come up to me and ask whether I've been part of an alcoholic support program. Somehow I must be carrying the message in my lectures. It's true I've brought a spiritual component into my lectures; I talk about how our bodies are divinely built by God. It might make some people uncomfortable, but a lot of people approach me after my lectures to tell me how much they connect with that spiritual aspect.

It certainly hasn't hurt my business. *Inc.* magazine listed CME4LIFE one of 2016's fastest-growing businesses in the country. Maybe that sounds like bragging, but I don't mean it that way. I am just so extremely grateful.

I'm grateful my company can help people. I'm grateful I can support my family. I'm grateful because I know all too well how badly things could have gone, but instead I've been blessed. I'm still very much a work in progress—and I will be until I die. I constantly have to check myself to make certain I'm not acting in a prideful or selfish way. I may not be drinking anymore, but I still have an alcoholic brain. Each day is a challenge; each day is a gift.

In January 2016, I was scheduled to receive my five-year sobriety coin. Each year since entering sobriety, I had asked Michelle if she would give me my coin. Each year, she'd turned me down. She hates public speaking to begin with, and she didn't want the embarrassment of standing in front of a group of strangers and talking about her husband being an alcoholic.

But when I asked her this time, she said yes. She had realized that it wasn't about her. It was about the poor guy three months into sobriety, his life and marriage falling apart, thinking he was about to lose everything—and then seeing someone five years in saying, "Yeah, we almost lost our family, but we didn't. You have to hang on to hope."

On the day of the ceremony, my nerves were in overdrive. Johnny, Matthew, and Sarah were there. My dad and mother-in-law came, too. I didn't know if I'd break down bawling.

There were a lot of guys called up before me, and the butterflies continued.

It's not about you, John. This is about giving other people hope and inspiration.

Finally, the announcer said, "Here is John with five years, and he'll be receiving his coin from his wife, Michelle."

Michelle stepped forward and gave a small smile. "When my husband first came to this group," she began, "I didn't know if he was really an alcoholic—or just an asshole."

Laughter rippled through the room, but tears welled in my eyes; she'd used those same words five years earlier. "I didn't know what was wrong with him," she continued, "but he grew here, and in many ways, I think he found God here. His faith has inspired me to find a deeper faith for myself. His walk of faith has been an inspiration to me."

Michelle took a deep breath and extended her hand, reaching out to me. "I'm giving John this coin today," she concluded. "But I think also this coin belongs to each of you and the support you've given him along his journey. I'm grateful you've given me back my husband's best self."

I smiled through my tears.

Afterword

I was a kid. *Six? Seven?* Trying to be all grown up and pour my own cup of milk. I missed and spilled it all over the floor. Milk was everywhere—on the counter, dripping down the cabinets, running like a white river across the floor. I stood there paralyzed, staring at the mess I'd made.

My father walked in and saw what I'd done. "What'd you do that for, Johnny?" he asked gruffly, grabbing some paper towels to help.

"Because I'm stupid," I replied sheepishly.

I had forgotten all about this until Dad reminded me of it recently. "You know," he said, "I've always felt bad about that. I should have corrected you—not for spilling the milk, but for calling yourself stupid. I should've told you that you weren't stupid."

I got a lump in my throat. The ways we think about ourselves—always, but especially from early on in life—affect us forever. I know what it's like to feel stupid. I know what it's like to feel like there's something to prove.

I've made a shit-ton of mistakes in my life—but I can't regret any of them. Because without those challenges, I wouldn't be where I am today. My failures and shortcomings have been a trapdoor to success.

I'm proud of being a Marine and serving my country;

when I hear the national anthem, I tear up, because I know I represented and fought for our country. I'm proud of my family. I'm proud of having pushed myself and stretched my limits, finishing marathons and an Ironman.

I'm proud of being a guy who didn't finish high school and yet went on to become a physician assistant, a teacher, and an international lecturer. I'm proud to have created and grown a business that helps other people expand their limits and fulfill their potential.

There's so much more I want to do.

I want to do the Lake Placid Ironman again. I owe that fucking race a finish. I look forward to living a life that prioritizes health, one in which going for a run or doing a CrossFit workout is as natural as brushing my teeth in the morning.

I have goals for my business, too. Here's just one: I want to lecture in front of an audience of five thousand people.

I also had a goal in writing this book: that through my story you will see that transformation is possible. When you're going through a shitty time in your life, I hope you're able to find something bigger than yourself and ask better questions. You may be asking, "Why did this happen *to* me?" I encourage you to ask: "Why did this happen *for* me? What am I supposed to learn from this? How am I supposed to grow from this?"

You must be honest with yourself, even when it's painful. It was certainly painful for me to revisit some of the stories I've told in this book. But I can't whitewash my truth. I have to be the circus clown following the elephants. I have to be willing to clean up my shit. I hope you will consider walking that path alongside me.

But above all, find your calling. For me, that means following God and doing His will. It means teaching and inspiring others. Not everyone hears the same voice, and that's fine. But there has to be a bigger power pulling you forward. Find that power. Find what you live for. People say to follow your passion—I say find your passion and attack it without mercy. The attack will reveal who you are: your gifts and your demons. Confront both.

If you don't like where you are in life, find a way to change it. You're responsible for your own life—the good and the bad. If you can't do it alone, find someone to help you. Find a coach, read a book. I learned so much through my twelve-step journey. I needed guides along the way; you likely do, too.

There's a story in the Gospel of Luke that's like an ember burning in my soul. It's about when Jesus entered Jerusalem before he was crucified. Outside of town, he sent some of his disciples ahead and told them they'd find a man with a donkey. "Tell the man the Lord needs the donkey, and he'll give it to you." When the disciples returned with the donkey, Jesus got on and made his triumphant entrance into Jerusalem.

After I heard that story, I couldn't stop thinking about the man who owned the donkey. He had a valuable donkey, and he just gave it away to some strangers, trusting that it was God's will. This man must have had such strong faith. He must have been willing to sacrifice anything and do whatever he could to serve God's plan. This story makes me wonder what my donkey is. I'm giving what I know I can give in service of my faith, but I still have more to give—and always will. What assets, skills, and talents can I contribute? What can I do to serve God's plan?

I'll keep living and working and waiting to hear.

Acknowledgments

My most important thanks goes to my wife, Michelle, for allowing me to undertake yet another project and having the courage to trudge this journey with me.

I'd like to thank Charles Beinhauer for giving me the inspiration to simply share my experience.

I want to thank my sister, Lisa Wheeler, for showing me the way. Your faith is a light.

I'd like to thank my CEO, Rick Scott, for his sage advice and support throughout this process.

I'd like to thank the team at RTC (Aleks, Geoff, Sarah, Kathy, Corey, et al.) for helping draw out my story and bring it to the page.

About the Author

John Bielinski, Jr. is the founder and owner of
CME4LIFE, LLC, an *Inc. 5000* company that teaches
clinical medicine, board preparation, and optimal
thinking. John holds a master of science degree in
family and emergency medicine and actively works as
an emergency medicine physician assistant in Western
New York. He lectures nationally on medical education.

As a child, John struggled in school, was labeled a
"difficult learner," and was placed in classes for students
with special needs. He never graduated high school.
He turned to martial arts and made fighting a way
of life. After a troubled youth, John joined the United
States Marine Corps, where he found discipline, seeing
front-line combat action during Operation Desert Storm.

Back home, John attended Erie Community College
and the University at Buffalo prior to graduating from
physician assistant's school at King's College. John
moved into clinical practice, working in emergency
medicine. He also developed a passion for teaching,
serving as an instructor for twelve years at two different
PA schools in Buffalo. John started lecturing nationally
and quickly became a favorite keynote speaker.

Married with kids and a faithful dog, with a
growing professional reputation, John competed in
full-contact kickboxing, ran numerous marathons,

and completed the Lake Placid Ironman Triathlon.

Although the struggle with his personal demons nearly cost him all of what he worked so hard to build, John founded CME4LIFE—now recognized as one of the nation's fastest-growing businesses—and is helping to train the next generation of physician assistants.

John is finally finding what eluded him his entire life—self-acceptance and inner peace. He's also deeply committed to helping those struggling with their own demons, healing the damage his demons caused others, and working to be the man he believes God is calling him to be.